Greening the Landscape

Greening the Landscape
Strategies for Environmentally Sound Practice

Adam Regn Arvidson

W. W. Norton & Company

New York • London

For information about permission to reproduce selections from this book, write to
Permissions, W. W. Norton & Company, Inc., 500 Fifth Avenue, New York, NY 10110

For information about special discounts for bulk purchases, please contact W. W. Norton
Special Sales at specialsales@wwnorton.com or 800-233-4830

Manufacturing by Courier Westford
Book design by Jonathan Lippincott
Electronic production by Joe Lops
Production manager: Leeann Graham

Library of Congress Cataloging-in-Publication Data

Arvidson, Adam Regn.
    Greening the landscape : strategies for environmentally sound practice / Adam Regn Arvidson.
— 1st ed.
        p. cm.
    Includes bibliographical references and index.
    ISBN 978-0-393-73353-2 (pbk.)
1. Landscape design—Environmental aspects.   I. Title.
    SB472.45.A78 2012
    712—dc23
                                                                    2012012393

ISBN: 978-0-393-73353-2 (pbk.)

W. W. Norton & Company, Inc., 500 Fifth Avenue, New York, N.Y. 10110
www.wwnorton.com
W. W. Norton & Company Ltd., Castle House, 75/76 Wells Street, London W1T 3QT

0 9 8 7 6 5 4 3 2 1

Contents

1: Making Landscapes Greener

Since the days of English manor gardens and Italian villas, landscapes have served as escapes from dirty, gray, close-quartered cities. At any scale—a backyard flower patch, a neighborhood open space, Central Park—these green oases offer some semblance of nature in the midst of a paved and built-upon world. Decades ago, describing them as "green" referred to little more than their color and their verdant character. Green areas were meant to contrast with extremely dense urban landscapes often choked with smog and without a growing thing in sight. Today, "green" means something entirely different. Major corporations are going green; green dry cleaning is widely available; even buildings and cars (the original foils to landscapes) are being built—and certified—as green as possible.

Today, green means environmentally sound. That is, of course, a loose measure, but plenty of industries are banking on the fact that greener practices can help the environment and potentially bring greater profits, because consumers seem to be very interested in being green.

Landscapes, of course, are green, not just in color but in environmental performance. It has always been true that landscape architects, nurseries, landscape contractors and management companies, parks departments, botanical gardens, corporations, and other creators and stewards of landscapes do bring some element of environmental benefit through most of the landscapes they design, build, and manage. Recent advances in landscape design have made landscapes even greener (in the environmental sense). Rain gardens, bioswales, and permeable pavement help manage storm-water runoff and its associated pollution. Green roofs reduce the heat island effect, increase the life of the roof itself, and reduce the heating and cooling costs of buildings. Interconnected parks, trails, and bikeways get more people on their feet, on their bikes, and out of their cars. Major prairie, forest, and wetland restorations within park systems and on college and corporate campuses reduce maintenance and provide habitats for plants and animals.

Because of the inherent greenness of landscapes, those who make and manage them are poised to have a significant positive impact on the environment. At a time when concerns about global climate change, river and coastal flooding, and dependence on foreign oil are at an all-time high, landscape professionals are also poised to capitalize on a worldwide wave of greenophilia. This is true at any scale, and environmental benefits can be realized in any landscape—from a residential redesign and installation, to the management of a citywide park system, to the design and construction of a major new landscape showpiece.

But what about that big delivery truck that brings plants to the site? How much fuel does it use? What about the skid-steer loaders (such as Bobcats) used to prepare the site for planting? Are they kicking out harmful emissions? And when the truck trundles away with all those plastic plant containers, where do they go?

And that's just during construction. Go back to the nursery and there are more questions. How much water and fertilizer is a grower using? And where do all those cuttings, prunings, and dead plants (the "green waste") end up? How about after construction? Is the project being maintained with a regimen of synthetic, petroleum-based fertilizers, herbicides, and pesticides? How much nitrous oxide is emitted by gas-driven hedge trimmers and leaf blowers? How much fuel is simply spilled by trying to top off those tiny engines with their tiny gas tanks?

Should growers, installers, managers, municipalities, universities, corporations, and landscape architects be more cognizant of these environmental effects? Should landscape architects use their design projects to encourage or require their landscape industry partners to be more environmentally sound? Should nurseries, installers, and management companies take the initiative to change their practices? Should corporations, universities, and parks departments strive to maintain their vast greenswards in a more environmentally friendly way? The answer to all these questions, of course, is yes.

But the most important question is this: How? How can nurseries, installers, and management companies go green when they are already typically operating with razor-thin profit margins? How can parks departments, corporations, and campuses alter their management practices while still providing aesthetically pleasing, functional landscapes? How can landscape architects, most of whom neither install nor manage landscapes, exert influence over their clients, their vendors, and a much larger and more ubiquitous landscape industry?

The simple answer to these questions goes back to how we measure "green." There are many shades of green, and all the creators and stewards of landscapes can pick the shade that is right for them at the moment. Change can be incremental and can build over time. This book outlines a wide variety of practices for making the installation and maintenance of landscapes more environmentally sound. They range from exceedingly simple ideas (like turning off engines when loading and unloading at a job site) to things that would take significant investment (building a new, high-tech, low-energy headquarters). The point is that anyone can do something. This book is a guide to the range of possibilities.

About this book

This book is for all the creators and stewards of landscapes. Anyone who designs, plans, installs, maintains, grows plants for, or otherwise cares for a landscape has some responsibility for doing so in a more environmentally friendly way. In partic-

ular this book addresses the practices of landscape architects and designers; of the so-called green industry, which includes nurseries, landscape contractors, and landscape management companies; and of the owners of large tracts of landscape: parks and recreation departments, state and federal agencies, universities, and corporations. Many of the principles outlined here could also be applied by homeowners, who, though they steward a smaller piece of land, still gas up mowers and fertilize lawns (and can make immediate changes, without reporting to a board or client).

Landscape architects. This book assumes throughout that landscape architects have a basic working knowledge of landscape architectural principles and methods, including specification writing. Beyond that, it will be understandable to all landscape architecture professionals and students who have ever prepared even a rudimentary planting plan or specification. It will offer guidance for practitioners from entry-level designers (for whom planting plans may be a regular task in an office setting) to seasoned experts (who often have "standard" specifications that, with a little modification, could improve a design's environmental performance).

The green industry. Throughout this book, "green industry" is a collective umbrella term for a variety of skilled professionals engaged in the creation, installation, and maintenance of softscapes, that is, plant material, as opposed to pavements, structures, and site furniture. The broadest categories of green industry professionals are nurseries, landscape contractors, and landscape management companies. True, landscape contractors are often responsible for hardscapes, as well, but this book focuses on the use of plants. This book does not provide an overview of standard nursery, landscape installation, or landscape management practices. Rather it offers guidance on how to change standard practices to improve environmental performance (and often reduce cost).

Landowners. This book makes little distinction between private owners (corporations that manage large campuses, private universities and colleges, and single-family homeowners) and public owners (parks and recreation departments, state and federal agencies, public colleges and universities, and other municipal landholders). Though each of these types of owners has a unique set of circumstances that govern their decision making on landscape management, the key topic here is in what way those management practices should change. As for green industry professionals, this book does not provide detail on standard landscape installation and management practices but instead recommends changes in those practices. It also does not address the logistics of procurement, other than to recommend ways of procuring more environmentally sound services in the context of public or private solicitations.

This is not a book on planting design. When first asked how to make landscapes more environmentally sound, most green industry professionals and landscape architects say, "put the right plant in the right place." In so doing, logically, the plant will thrive and require less water, less fertilizer, and fewer "inputs." There are numerous books on landscape design published every month, which can help with understanding what plants to use in particular regions. This book will help to ensure that the plants and the manner in which they get put in the ground are more environmentally sound.

This book also does not spend time specifically on rain gardens, green roofs, storm-water swales, or other new green landscape technologies. Though environmentally sound, those landscapes may still utilize plants in plastic pots, may still require unnecessary amounts of vehicle fuel to install, and may still replace existing landscaping that is subsequently landfilled rather than composted. Therefore, these landscape types are treated here like any other landscape.

This book is meant to help modify, in an environmentally friendly way, any design, installation, or management practice—by looking not at the plants themselves but at how those plants are grown, installed, and maintained. This book deals with making the everyday landscape—the kind of commercial, residential, or municipal projects that the creators and stewards of landscapes deal with all the time—more sustainable by changing methods and practices.

After this introductory chapter, seven more chapters follow. Chapters 2 through 6 deals with one of the five major environmental impacts of design, installation, and management of landscapes: plant pots, vehicle fuel, energy consumption, water and fertilizer, and green waste. Each of these chapters provides a general overview of the issue and some ideas for mitigating impact. Accompanying these chapters are multiple case studies from across the United States, profiling green industry companies and landscape architects that have already made strides in certain areas and therefore have proved that change is possible.

At the conclusion of each of these five chapters is a checklist with specific ideas that could be put to use right away. The checklists describe specific actions that owners, green industry professionals, and landscape architects can perform to increase the environmental credibility of their landscapes. The actions are organized according to the tools described in this chapter: plans and specifications, working with green industry professionals, changing internal practices, and advocacy.

In general, the actions regarding plans and specifications and working with green industry professionals are geared toward landscape architects and owners. The changing internal practices actions are for green industry professionals themselves, as well as for owners that perform installation and management tasks with their own crews. This is particularly true of parks departments and college campuses. The advocacy actions apply across the board.

Chapter 7 considers landscapes in the context of today's established environmental rating systems, such as the U.S. Green Building Council's Leadership in Energy and Environmental Design (LEED) and the Sustainable Sites Initiative (SITES). Most rating systems provide credit for the items recommended in the environmental impacts chapters, and achieving credits can provide additional incentive to some clients, owners, and green industry companies.

Chapter 8 summarizes all the checklists in the environmental impacts chapters, because many of the recommended changes can improve environmental health in multiple ways. This last chapter constitutes the critical list of tasks a municipality, corporation, green industry professional, or landscape architect can take on to improve the performance of their landscapes, organized according to how exactly the project is getting built and managed, with input on public bids, custom-grown plants, contractor selection, and so on.

The environmental impacts of landscapes

Before considering what can be done it is important to first briefly consider the environmental impact of making and managing landscapes. Note that in this book I rely on terms like "environmental impact," "environmentally sound," and "environmental credibility" as opposed to "sustainability." This is because, though it is often used to reference the environment, "sustainability" has gained much broader meaning as a total measure of a company's, product's, or landscape's success on environmental, social, and economic fronts. This book is focused on improving environmental performance, so sustainability would be too broad a word. In some cases there can be resultant economic and social benefit from the ideas discussed here, but in these pages the environment comes first. The environmental impacts of landscapes fall into five broad categories.

Plant pots. The vast majority of the time, plastic plant pots end up in landfills. Though recycling programs have been a focus of several state professional organizations, recycling is not the nationwide norm. This is due to many factors, among which is the fluctuating price of oil and plastic. The Illinois Green Industry Association (IGIA) has been trying to start a recycling program for seven years, according to that trade group's executive director, Dave Bender, with little success, despite the support expressed by its members through special meetings and surveys. In 2009, under pressure from the local press, the IGIA set up a collection day when nurseries and installers could bring used pots in for free recycling. Not one company registered, so the event was cancelled.[1] The big problem is that most recyclers want pots to be washed clean. Most landscape industry professionals simply cannot bear the time and effort to do this. So the typical plant container is made from virgin plastic, used to house one plant, then buried in the earth or incinerated.

Vehicle fuel. Pickup trucks, dump trucks, skidsteers, mowers, and blowers all use fossil fuels, which contribute to greenhouse gas emissions. There isn't much information, however, on how much fuel it takes to get a project in the ground. Standard pickup trucks run anywhere between twelve and twenty-one miles per gallon in the city (the larger, "workhorse" construction pickups, of course, fall on the low end of that spectrum). That efficiency drops further when the truck is pulling a trailer—a common event for a landscape installer or manager. Another basic rule: the higher the horsepower, the lower the fuel efficiency, so using the smallest possible machine can help reduce both emissions and costs. Yet many contractors are small companies, with only a few pieces of construction equipment, so they tend to buy extra horsepower for the few occasions they will need it. Nurseries and growers use vehicles to move around their growing yards: pickups and skidsteers are common here, too.

When it comes to construction equipment, the Environmental Protection Agency (EPA) regulates emissions, not fuel efficiency, though in small engines the two often go hand-in-hand. The EPA specifically looks at hydrocarbons (HC), nitrogen oxides (NOx), and carbon monoxide (CO). According to the EPA, in 2008, when the most recent standards were implemented, the small-spark-ignition category, which includes most lawn maintenance equipment, and marine engines, made up 25 percent of volatile organic compound emissions and 23 percent of carbon monoxide emissions from all vehicles (yes, including automobiles).

Regulation divides the workhorses of landscaping—skidsteers, mini excavators, riding mowers, blowers, and trimmers—into two groups: small-spark-ignition engines (25 horsepower and less) like those in mowers and handheld maintenance equipment, and nonroad diesel engines, which are found in the bigger construction equipment. The EPA has regularly improved standards, ever since Congress required it to regulate nonroad vehicle emissions under the Clean Air Act of 1990. Equipment manufacturers have been forced to improve their equipment over time, primarily by phasing out dirty two-stroke engines. However, regulations roll in by model year and older equipment can be prevalent on job sites. (There is more about regulations in chapter 4.)[2]

Energy consumption. In addition to the fuel that growers, contractors, and management companies use is the power it takes to run their home bases. This is especially the case with growers, which must heat and aerate greenhouses almost year-round, even in the nursery mecca of Oregon, where winter plantings require interior heating. Greenhouses—typically made of one-ply plastic stretched over a metal framework—are inherently inefficient. Offices for landscape contractors and management companies are most often located in utilitarian warehouses, which are difficult to heat in the winter and cool in the summer.

Water and fertilizer. To water plants, most nurseries draw up well water and spray it over acres of plants with high-mounted irrigation heads. Sometimes fertilizer is added to the mix before spraying. Water that doesn't evaporate or land on plants hits the ground, runs off, and reenters the groundwater or adjacent watercourses. In many rural counties (prime locations for nurseries), there are few rules governing the runoff, so it may see little if any treatment. Fertilizers—even those added to soil rather than to the irrigation water—may go right along with it, since they are designed to be water-soluble so plants can drink them. Whatever the plant can't take up stays in the water to fertilize other things downstream, like algal blooms that threaten marine life. In addition, according to Whitney Rideout of the Oregon Association of Nurseries, fertilizer is a "huge energy user."[3] Synthetic fertilizer is typically petroleum based and both the fuel and the fertilizer itself must be transported over long distances.

The combination of water and fertilizer is also a key aspect of landscape management, and some of the issues are the same as in a nursery. Water is often wasted by irrigation systems with set programs rather than with weather- and moisture-adaptable regimes. Fertilizers, pesticides, and herbicides are typically synthetic and petroleum based. Fertilizer and water are rarely reused, so they run off, which costs money and can cause environmental damage. These issues become more complex than at a nursery, however, because the management of a site is a task most often shared by an owner and a contracted management company. Though many parks systems, botanical gardens, and university campuses are maintained by dedicated crews, the vast majority of commercial and large residential sites involve decision making by two parties: one actually doing the work, and one paying for the work. Bringing better environmental performance to water and fertilizers requires an owner willing to push the envelope (sometimes paying a bit more for that privilege) and a management company that either is familiar with environmental techniques or is willing to learn.

Ultimately, the millions and millions of acres of maintained landscapes have significant ongoing environmental impact due to the amounts of water and fertilizer that are used. This is especially true in the arid southwest, where water must be brought from very far away and where runoff often travels overland rather than sinking into the soil to be filtered.

Green waste. Green waste—the mixture of soil and plants generated by nurseries and installers—often goes to a landfill. This waste is compostable, but that takes time, money, and trouble, so it is generally not done unless there is specific state regulation. Only twenty-four states (see the list on page XXX) forbid some or all landscape waste in landfills. And the current trend is to roll back such no-landfill laws. In 2011 Michigan barely escaped a repeal, and Florida and Georgia did just eliminate their mandatory composting laws, in 2010 and 2011, respectively.[3] The reason for these repeals is often stated by waste management companies to be the additional production of electricity generated from landfill methane. The more stuff in the landfill, the logic goes, the more electricity there will be. Green waste, though, makes up a small fraction of total landfill solids, so the United States Composting Council (USCC) reasons that the real motivator is increased income from landfill fees and from curbside pick-up efficiencies. The USCC, however, counts member composting facilities in every state but six, and there are surely many more small composting companies or municipal facilities available to nurseries, contractors, and management companies.

Why change? and how?

Research suggests that humans are altering the Earth's climate in a way never seen before. The main cause of global climate change is greenhouse gases created by the burning of fossil fuels. Vehicles, buildings, and industrial practices account for the largest share of emissions. Comparatively, the landscape architecture profession and the green industry have minimal effect, but the problem of climate change can only be solved through comprehensive change at all levels of society and industry. In addition, the creation and management of land-scapes does have significant potential local effects, such as runoff fouling salmon streams in the Pacific Northwest, nursery and landscape irrigation draining lakes and aquifers in the arid southwest, and a glut of landfilled plastic pots wherever recycling programs do not exist.

It is true that change can be hard on a small business, which may lack the capital to invest in things like solar panels, energy-efficient renovations, or hybrid vehicles. However, there are numerous changes that can actually save owners and green industry professionals money in the long run. Changing out older maintenance equipment or using more hand maintenance can save money on fuel and equipment upkeep. Nurseries that effectively manage their irrigation water could reuse that water—right along with the fertilizer it still contains. Owners could cut material costs, and management companies could cut labor costs by using potless annuals. There are examples in this book of these practices actually being performed in the industry. Landscape architects and public policy makers may also play a role in making the cost argument moot, especially on public projects. By requiring all bidders to do the same things—reduce idling, recycle pots and waste, control emissions—all bidders will need to make the same investment. This also incentivizes the early adoption of environmental practices.

Landscape architects pride themselves on being environmentally aware, and many recent advancements in landscape architecture are having positive effects on environmental health. Green-minded companies promote their environmental accomplishments in the production of their wares. Parks departments claim to be stewards of the natural landscape. College campuses serve a population for whom the environment is a key issue. Green industry professionals (in addition to boasting a suddenly prescient name) are, in fact, growing, installing, and maintaining highly beneficial plants. Why not, then, extend this environmental credibility beyond general marketing language or the broad goals of a design project and into installation and maintenance practices themselves? The creators and stewards of landscapes have four broad tools for effecting environmental improvement.

Plans and specifications. Designers control every aspect of many projects with detailed plans and written specifications—every aspect, that is, they desire to control. A landscape architect would never issue a set of signed plans without pavement cross sections, but it is rarely ever noted what kind of vessel a plant should come in. "Container grown" is a common notation on plans and in specifications—the assumption being that this will be a plastic pot. But landscape architects can require more environmentally sound practices, both at the front end and the back end. For instance, a designer could specify something other than a plastic pot: bare-root shrubs, say, or some alternative material, like peat or paper (more on that in chapter 2). Additionally, they could require certain submittals to verify environmentally sound practices after installation, like pot recycling or composting. Any collection facility will offer a receipt, which could become a required project submittal, just as contractors typically must submit information on plant material origin, concrete batch data and test results, and other items.

All this is also true of public and corporate policy makers. Staff at parks departments, departments of transportation, corporation design offices, and campus management departments all have some responsibility for the standard contracts by which their organizations set out work expectations. Changing standard specifications could affect an entire state's roadway system, say, or a college campus comprising hundreds of acres. Such staff also have the benefit of being able to control practices both in installation and management after the fact (something over which a contracted landscape architect may have little say). By creating new or altering standard plans and specifications to address the installation, maintenance, and, where possible, plant growing, landscape designers and owners can have more influence over the total environmental health of their projects.

Working with green industry companies. For private-sector jobs—those residential and commercial landscapes that are the bread and butter of so many landscape architecture firms—a designer often has some say in the selection of green industry professionals. Landscape architects are always asked to recommend contractors, many of whom are happy to stay on the job for a regular maintenance regimen. By understanding the environmentally sound practices available within the green industry, landscape architects either can select those firms already engaging in some of those practices or can work with companies to change their practices, in exchange for future recommendations and opportunities to bid on the designer's projects.

Similarly, site managers at corporations (and sometimes at campuses or parks departments, though these organizations may have in-house maintenance staff) often can freely select installation and management companies. They may also form long-term relationships with certain companies and can work with them to change practices over time. It is unlikely that any landscape contractor or management company will be tackling all the environmental ideas contained in this book, but by building relationships with installers, managers, and nurseries—something many landscape architects and owners already do—those green industry professionals can be encouraged to edge toward greener practices.

Changing internal practices. Nurseries, landscape contractors, landscape managers, and site owners that maintain their own properties could have potentially the greatest effect on the environmental performance of landscapes. By changing their own internal practices—by upgrading old equipment, by composting green waste even in areas where that is not required by law, or by using rainwater for irrigation—owners and green industry companies could change the ways landscapes are grown, installed, and maintained.

Of course, some of these things will cost money up front. They will also require an investment of time—something often in short supply for these companies, especially during the warm season. However, as demonstrated by Pacific Landscape Management (see the case study in chapter 3) and the resources being created by the Oregon Association of Nurseries (see the second case study in chapter 4), some environmental practices can actually save a parks department, landscape contractor, botanical garden, or landscape management company real money—almost immediately. Collectively, the green industry is the largest group among those discussed in this book. It also is the only group able to effect change at every stage of the landscape creation and management process—from plants grown in the nursery to regular maintenance practices after installation.

Advocacy. All owners, green industry professionals, and landscape architects can work to change policies at the local, state, and national level. Some municipalities have standard requirements that could be improved from an environmental standpoint. Just as many large cities require contractors to pay employees a "prevailing wage," those cities could require, for instance, pot recycling, green-waste composting, or equipment meeting the most recent EPA emissions standards. Landscape architects and green industry professionals in both the public and private sectors are trusted resources when it comes to landscape installation and maintenance, and they are poised to encourage change in public policies. Advocacy is particularly important when municipal regulations prevent best environmental practices.

The use of these four tools will vary considerably by jurisdiction. In Minnesota, for instance, there is no reason to campaign for green-waste composting or even to write that requirement into a specification. In Florida, however, landscape architects and green industry professionals could advocate for it, at the same time they write the requirement into their specifications or adopt composting as a standard practice. The choice of whether to regulate through project drawings, carefully select and negotiate with an installer or manager, change internal practices, or advocate for change will depend on the type of professional, the project, and the client. Owners, landscape architects, growers, installers, and managers, though, can use these four broad tools to improve the overall environmental performance of their landscapes.

Christy Webber, head of a Chicago landscape company (see the first case study in chapter 4), once said, "The green industry thinks it's green because it plants trees." But she believes that's not enough, and she's not alone. Landscapes have always been considered green—and they are. But they could be greener.

Improving environmental practices will require symbiotic relationships among green industry professionals, site owners, and landscape architects. Such relationships may have many faces. A campus landscape architect could modify standard specifications to improve the environmental performance of new installations and ongoing maintenance. A large corporation's site development arm could develop a new process for selecting regional contractors based on their environmental credibility. A landscape architect could require various environmental practices in a specification issued for public bid. A parks department could upgrade its maintenance equipment or perform more hand maintenance. A nursery could steam and reuse its pots or install more efficient greenhouse coverings. A landscape contractor could convert to biodiesel or hybrid trucks. A landscape manager could experiment with organic fertilizers.

The most important task, though, is changing our collective mind-set. It is simply not enough to create more landscapes—even environmentally innovative ones like rain gardens or green roofs. All the creators and stewards of landscapes should understand that landscapes do not have inherent environmental credibility. How they are installed and maintained is just as important as how much storm water they treat, how many native species they are home to, and how much carbon they sequester. A landscape that sends plastic pots and green waste to landfills, requires large amounts of fuel to install and maintain, is fertilized with petroleum-based chemicals, or features plants grown with excessive water and fertilizer cannot be considered truly green, no matter its ongoing environmental performance. A green landscape begins with the seed in the nursery and continues through every trimming and mowing. This is true no matter the site ownership, landscape type, or design style. All creators and stewards of landscapes should have a hand in making landscapes greener.

CASE STUDY: ONE GREEN WORLD

The Portland, Oregon, area is known for its environmental practices. Most of the region's vaunted initiatives, though, tend to be urban: an extensive light-rail transportation system, growth boundaries that help prevent suburban sprawl, innovative storm-water management systems integrated into city streets, and more green roofs than almost anywhere else. Oregon is also a major nursery state—it's third in the nation in the production of ornamental and landscape plants, behind only California and Florida—and some of its growers are also embracing green thinking.

One Green World (OGW) is a modest sixty-six-acre nursery focused on edible plants for the landscape. The thirty-plus-year-old company grows everything from the old standards like apples, cherries, and blueberries to strange food plants like paw paw, goji berry, and salal. It feels a bit like a farm market, set well off the main road, featuring a gravel parking lot and a long wood and steel shed out of which OGW sells direct to drop-in customers.

The office is fairly typical: a bit overcrowded and cluttered, plant posters and hardiness zone maps taped to the walls, old

The biodiesel-powered soil steamer at One Green World allows the nursery to reuse spent potting soil and plant pots. (Northwoods Nursery / One Green World)

computers graying with age and dust, a linoleum floor seemingly permanently stained with ground-in dirt. Just outside the office door, though, is the steamer. OGW reuses its spent potting mix—the soil left in the pots when plants are transplanted or prepared for shipping. Such reuse is rare in the industry, as plants can leave pathogens behind and the soil can sicken new plants if it is used as is. OGW's setup includes a low box with a tarp lid. Hoses enter from the back, delivering heated water vapor (steam) from a machine just beside the box. Blowers push the steam into the box and the soil is, in essence, sterilized. OGW's standard soil mix is a combination of shredded bark, humus, and peat, and the company now fills new pots with one-quarter steamed soil and three-quarters fresh soil (without testing all the steamed soil, it is hard to know how much fertilizer remains in that soil; mixing it with new soil allows OGW to better regulate fertilizer content).

The steamer also works on pots, so OGW tries to reuse all the pots they can. In fact, the company has partnered with the nearby Oregon City waste collection facility to collect plastic pots from landscapers in the area, in addition to taking pots back from its customers. Behind the greenhouses, near the compost pile, a mountain of pots awaits sorting. The undamaged pots will be steamed and potted with new edible plants, and the rest will go to a local recycler.

OGW composts all its green waste. The company piles all its cuttings, clippings, and even old trees and shrubs in a wooden enclosure that looks like a stable, complete with different bays for different stages of the composting process. A chipper is on hand for woody materials, and OGW's neighbor, a horse boarding facility, provides regular deliveries of manure on a dedicated farm road that connects the two properties. The green waste, woody material, and manure is mixed and allowed to decompose, then used primarily on the nursery's "mother blocks," stands of mature food plants from which OGW takes propagation cuttings to make new plants for sale. The compost serves as both fertilizer and weed suppression for these precious and coddled plants.

Addressing green waste, spent soil, and plastic pots constitutes one of three broad environmental focus areas for OGW: the waste stream. The company is also looking at energy consumption and crop practices. In the latter area OGW has eliminated pre-emergent herbicides in their plant pots. Every plant pot gets a top dressing of locally produced bark mulch (Oregon is also a major producer of forest products) and may be hand weeded if weeds still appear in the pots. Eliminating herbicides saves money, of course, but the mulching, though it seems labor intensive, actually saves about $40,000 in later weeding costs.

In the outdoor growing yards, where plants are started in the ground rather than in pots, OGW puts sawdust mulch at the plants' feet in their long rows, under which runs T-tape drip irrigation. The tape is inexpensive and easily moved, unlike permanent pipe systems. It wears out after two or three years and is recycled along with damaged plant pots and spent greenhouse roofing. The drip irrigation delivers water and fertilizer (currently synthetic, but OGW has in the past and continues to experiment with organic fertilizers) directly to plant roots, and the sawdust keeps the moisture in the soil for longer. OGW also plants cover crops like perennial ryegrass between the rows, in order to keep weeds down and reduce the need for herbicides or mowing. And, perhaps counterintuitively for a company with limited space and hundreds of species to propagate and grow, some of these fields are left fallow on a regular rotation. They are planted with cereal crops and legumes to put nitrogen back in the soil and left to recharge for a growing season, then put back to use.

OGW is also looking at adjusting its growing season to come more in line with the actual weather. Currently, in order to meet spring demand, plants are started in the winter—indoors. Lorraine Gardner, one of OGW's owners, feels that if plants could get their start the previous summer, go dormant in winter or overwinter in sheltered areas, then be ready for sale in the spring, the company could cut down on energy costs. Of course it would take more time to grow a plant, she says, "but that would be time in an unheated greenhouse."

OGW's greenhouses are pretty typical at first glance: a

One Green World uses drip irrigation in its growing fields, which are buried in sawdust mulch.

long tunnel of plastic supported by metal poles, gravel underfoot, a huge blower above the door. Gardner had to point out the differences. The roof is actually a double layer of plastic with an air pocket in between, which provides better insulation. The doors, the most permeable part of a greenhouse, are triple-ply plastic and are gasketed around the edges to prevent

All of One Green World's greenhouses feature radiant heating.
(Northwoods Nursery / One Green World)

and in these the radiant system runs on the underside of the tables. Gardner says that when the system is up and running in every greenhouse, in combination with the other efficiencies in greenhouse construction, OGW could save 50 percent on its heating costs.

Most transportation within the site is done on bicycle. Gardner says that a couple of years ago the company realized that most of the running around from one greenhouse to another, from growing field to office, didn't involve any hauling. Rather, staff was heading to one place with a pair of shears to do some pruning, then zooming over to a growing field to start up the irrigation, then returning to the office for break time or lunch. And they were doing it in motorized vehicles. Today, bicycles roam the premises, with plastic crates mounted to them for carrying tools, a stack of pots, or other small items.

Of course, not all errands can happen by bike, but OGW has reduced fossil fuel usage in the big equipment, too. The motor on the soil and pot steamer runs on biodiesel, as do the delivery van, a skidsteer, all the tractors save one, and the off-site "plantmobile," which periodically delivers orders into Portland and Eugene to reduce customer car trips out to the nursery. The company uses B99 (99 percent vegetable oil) in the summer and switches to B50 (50 percent vegetable oil)

warm air from escaping. And beneath the gravel is a radiant heating system, highly unusual in a greenhouse. The advantage here is that the heat comes from beneath, where the plants actually are, so it is more efficient in keeping the actual plants—rather than just the greenhouse air—warm. Some OGW greenhouses have raised metal tables for smaller plants,

A massive cistern stores rain- and irrigation water at One Green World.

storage tank that can hold one acre-foot of water (that's more than 325,000 gallons). Oregon is known as a rainy place, but the summers can actually be quite dry, so OGW is working on capturing winter and spring rainwater to use later. The company's 2.25-acre "Cravo house" (a retractable-roofed unheated greenhouse) has elevated micromist irrigation and also an underdrain system to capture runoff. Previously that runoff went into holding ponds, then grassy ditches, before being sent to a local creek. But now it is pumped into that big cistern to be reused for irrigation. The underdrains capture rainfall and irrigation water, so in the wet months, OGW can stock up on water to use in the dry season; then all the irrigation overshot is sent back to the cistern for another round of watering. OGW hopes to handle almost all of its watering with this cistern, eventually using its deep well only for emergencies.

OGW's sole drawback is that it sells only edible plants. Sure, these are nice in the landscape, too, but OGW doesn't grow maple or liriope or a spirea. If it did, landscape architects, installers, and owners could rest assured that those plants would be green from seed onward.

in the winter, when cold temperatures can turn biodiesel to sludge. The vegetable oil is left over from frying potato chips at the huge Kettle Chips factory in Salem, Oregon.

The shiniest, newest addition to the nursery is a massive

2: Planting Pots: A Life-Cycle Problem

It is one of the most familiar aspects of landscape construction. Perhaps it is too familiar: the plastic plant pot. There's the classic #1 for perennials, #5s and #10s for shrubs, and even #25s for smaller trees. At any nursery or growing yard they line up in neat rows, stretching across the landscape, one plant per pot. It is nearly impossible to determine how many plastic plant pots are used per year, but consider this. In 2011, a single Chicago-area grower of perennials, Midwest Groundcovers, produced 12.7 million plants. That's 12.7 million plastic pots, of various shapes and sizes. According to its website, the ubiquitous manufacturer Monrovia (which markets itself by emblazoning its name on its green pots) grows more than 20 million plants annually.[1] A #1 pot is about six inches in diameter; when stacked, each pot is about an inch higher than the next one down. That means the combined output of just these two referenced nurseries would cover a football field nearly twelve feet deep. A single stack of about 33 million pots would reach up to five hundred miles into the sky—well beyond the earth's atmosphere

It is very difficult to purchase a plant without its petrochemical container, especially in the nursery industry. A landscape architect specifying a plant without a pot is apt to get incredulous looks from contractors—and those same contractors may get those same looks from plant suppliers if they ask about alternatives to plastic.

The main problem with plastic plant pots is that they rarely are made from recycled plastic. They are also difficult to recycle. Though just about every single one of them will have a little number on its bottom, encircled with the friendly recycling arrows, it has always been notoriously problematic for anyone to turn them into new pots, drink bottles, or other recycled plastic products.

Most plant pots and nursery flats are made from high-density polyethylene (HDPE), that's number 2; polypropylene (PP), number 5; or polystyrene (PS), number 6. All of these materials are recyclable, but most recyclers don't want plant pots because they include plenty of impurities: the dirt that clings to the inside of the pots and is difficult to remove. All that dirt can cause problems in the recycling stream, unlike drink bottles, whose residue is liquid and easily washed away.

The difficulty of processing these pots has been typically passed along to those dropping off the pots. For instance, the recycling program operated by Midwest Groundcovers (see the case study in chapter 5) requires pots to be dry, clean, and free of any loose soil. That means an installer, rather than tipping a plant out of the pot, stacking the pot on the truck, and dumping the stack in the garbage, now must clean each pot and sort the stack by the number on the bottom. The Minnesota Nursery and Landscape Association (MNLA) program (see this chapter's case study) doesn't require the pots to be cleaned or sorted, but they still have to be free of dirt, rocks, and attached plant tags. In all cases, an installer has to truck the pots to a different location than other garbage. All that preparation, sorting, and delivery, of course, increases a contractor's time and costs.

Reduce, reuse, recycle

The best way to reduce the number of plant pots that end up in the landfill is to reduce the number of plant pots used on each job. That is not to say landscapes should feature fewer plants in order to save landfill space; rather, landscape architects and owners should consider carefully when plant pots are truly necessary (alternative materials are discussed in the next section). Bare-root trees and shrubs are a good alternative in many instances. Smaller trees, in particular, which may come in #25 plastic containers, are good candidates for bare-root planting. Of course, this requires more care in the field and careful scheduling, but these plants are often less expensive than potted plants. Large shrub massings, especially those not at the front and center of a project, could also be bare-root planted.

In some cases, plastic plant pots can be reused in their current form, without being recycled. In its recycling program, Midwest Groundcovers pulls certain pots out to reuse at its facility. The company simply knocks out loose soil and plants new stock—though not crops that are sensitive to root diseases. At One Green World, a steamer cleanses pots for reuse and the company also accepts customers' pots, essentially receiving free pots for reuse.

Recycling programs are beginning to catch on in certain

places. Most often, this requires a carefully executed agreement between a trade association, local nurseries, and a recycling company. Few major growers or landscaping companies have themselves taken on the task of starting up a program—the exceptions being Midwest Groundcovers and the MNLA.

One industry leader in Michigan, East Jordan Plastics (EJP), is collecting plant pots and recycling them into brand-new plant pots. The company, which has been in business since the 1940s, says it is committed to a closed loop system whereby all the pots in the midwestern United States are transformed into new plant pots. EJP calls this initiative "Project 100%" and the company is actively seeking plastic to recycle, which is unusual in the industry. EJP collects from the Home Depot and Meijer garden center locations in the Midwest; accepts pots at its South Haven, Michigan, recycling facility; and will even coordinate pickups around the Midwest (as pickups only or with the delivery of new plant pots).[2] The Michigan location of Midwest Groundcovers, in fact, transports all its pots to EJP and buys all its new pots from EJP, proving that the closed loop is a true possibility.

Alternative products

There are options out there besides plastic, but none has been embraced on a large scale in the nursery industry. Iron-ically, this is likely due to the durability of the plastic pot. Despite the fact that it will most often be used for one plant that is then tossed, a plant pot needs to be strong, because it is typically shuttled multiple times around a growing field, loaded onto trucks, exposed to the elements, and overall handled roughly. Pots made from peat, manure, and biodegradable vegetable matter haven't proven to have an equivalent toughness.

However, some growers, especially smaller specialty growers of native plants, are embracing other materials, generally using environmentally sensitive, smaller (four-inch) pots for seedlings and plugs. Perhaps the most well-known plastic pot alternative is the peat pot. Peat pots can be planted with the plants, because they break down in the soil and even offer nutrients to the plants. There's no need to recycle or landfill them. However, peat is generally considered a nonrenewable resource. Peat is partially decayed vegetable matter that builds up in wet landscapes like bogs and marshes. The vegetation fails to decay because it remains saturated in the ground and thickly compressed, which prevents air intrusion. Peat grows about only one millimeter per year and contains large amounts of carbon, which is expelled into the atmosphere when peat is harvested or burned for energy.[3] One landscape peat producer in Canada has achieved Veriflora certification (see chapter 7), suggesting more sustainable harvesting methods that include some preservation.[4]

Cow pots look a lot like peat pots but they are made from, you guessed it, cow manure. For the commercial grower, cow pots are marketed as seed-starting vessels, potentially replacing small peat pots or plastic starter trays.[5] Cow manure is assuredly a renewable resource.

Another alternative to plastic is vegetable fiber. Several makers of these pots market to both the consumer, with decorative outdoor pots, and the grower, with more utilitarian models. Ecoforms uses rice hulls and starch-based binding agents, and it claims not to use any pollutants at any manufacturing stage. The company grew from a Northern California nursery business that was initially concerned with its own plastic pot use. Ecoforms recommends composting at an established composting facility and that the pots should be tossed in with the green waste (see chapter 6).[6] Rosso's International is making brightly colored pots out of Chinese bamboo, the fastest-growing plant in the world.[7] These are primarily aimed at the consumer, so they may not be available by request in the landscape industry. Rush Creek Designs uses rice husks and bamboo to entice, again, primarily consumers.[8]

A recent breakthrough originally developed in Denmark eliminates the pot entirely. The Ellepot® is essentially a paper cylinder filled with a planting medium. Cylinders are placed in plastic trays that can be refilled with new Ellepots. Pacific Landscape Management (see the case study in chapter 3) began purchasing annuals in Ellepots at the request of a site owner and found them to be not only environmentally preferable to plastic but also faster (and therefore cheaper) to plant, since the plants do not have to be removed from pots. The Danish company Ellegaard holds a worldwide patent and sells machines to wholesalers and nurseries across the globe. With an Ellepot machine, any business can make its own pots, either for sale to growers and nurseries or for use in its own operations. The soil blend is customizable, meaning Ellepots can be filled with proprietary soil mixes or soil types appropriate to particular regions or plant needs.[9] The size of an Ellepot is a limiting factor, ensuring this technology will be useful for propagation in nurseries and the planting of smaller plants—annuals, perennial plugs, vegetables—but not for the use of larger landscape plants like shrubs or gallon perennials.

CHECKLIST

Creating plans and specifications

❑ **Specify more bare-root plants.** Obviously, the more bare-root trees and shrubs that are installed in landscapes, the fewer the plastic pots utilized. Bare-root planting does require more careful timing of installation and ordering, so it may not be appropriate in all situations, but, especially on projects with large massings of species, or in restoration projects, this can be a cost-effective option.

❑ **Specify field-grown and balled-and-burlapped trees.** Some smaller ornamental trees are commonly delivered in large (#25) plastic containers. In addition to sitting in a large virgin plastic pot, such trees may also have encircling roots or be root-bound. Choosing either slightly larger trees of the same species, so they are balled and burlapped, or simply specifying field-dug, balled-and-burlapped trees, can reduce unnecessary (and large) plastic pots.

❑ **Specify alternatives to plastic pots.** True, the industry standard is the plastic pot, and it may be difficult and costly to require something different. However, in some situations, especially large projects with significant numbers of plants, owners and landscape architects could work with growers and installers to use an alternative product.

This is also a good option when plants are custom-grown, either because of a project's size or because the project requires hard-to-find species.

❑ **Require plastic recycling.** In the submittals section of a typical specification, especially one for public bid, a variety of documentation is required of a contractor. Everything from concrete strength tests to plant provenance to aggregate gradations can be documented and submitted to the landscape architect or owner's representative for approval or as proof of certain practices. This is true of specifications created by landscape architects for a certain project, specifications considered "standard" within a design office, and an owner's corporate, campus, or agency standard specifications. If a plastics recycling facility or an optional recycling program exists in the area (like the one in Minnesota), project and standard specifications could require the drop-off of all used pots as well as documentation of that drop-off. Recycling facilities can offer some type of receipt for drop-off, as can a coordinated recycling program on request. Penalties could also be written into the specification, as they are for inadvertent tree removal or unacceptable time delays, for failure to recycle pots or document the drop-off. Certainly this will be a new requirement for most contractors, so they should be alerted to it at the beginning of a job, or even at bidding, since they may wish to build in nominal cost for any drop-off fees, for administration, and for cleaning and sorting. As to the concern for increased costs, if this rule is written into the specification for public bid, all contractors should have the same cost. And ultimately, the cost to drop off pots at a recycling facility instead of a construction landfill should be minimal relative to the overall cost of the project.

Working with green industry professionals

❑ **Ask installers to recycle used pots.** On private projects, landscape architects often have some say over what company will be installing their work. At the very least, most owners ask for recommendations, from which bids are requested. In such a bidding climate, landscape contractors know they must form a good working relationship with designers, in order to be recommended for future projects. Private owners may solicit multiple bids but can select a vendor based on factors other than cost. An owner or landscape architect might change an installer's standard practice by simply asking an installer to recycle and providing some resources on how to do so.

❑ **Choose and recommend installers with environmen-** tal credibility. Landscape contractors rely for part of their business on recommendations from owners and design professionals. Those customers, therefore, can make it clear that they will recommend primarily contractors with strong environmental pedigrees, or those who are working toward improved environmental sustainability. Recycling as a standard practice could be one of the factors governing that recommendation. (See "Questions for installers" in chapter 8.)

❑ **Work with growers that reuse or recycle.** Some growers (such as One Green World) are already reusing plastic pots as is, which is even better than recycling. Others, like Midwest Groundcovers, have a recycling program for which they bear the majority of the costs. Plants from growers like these are more environmentally sustainable when it comes to plastic use. In certain cases, especially if plants are being custom grown or on private jobs where a designer or owner has a lot of say over installation, it may be possible to choose where a project's plants are grown. When this is the case, growers can be selected based on overall environmental credibility, of which plastic pot reuse and recycling is a part. (See "Questions for growers" in chapter 8.)

❑ **Request alternative materials.** Pacific Landscape Management buys annuals from a grower that uses Ellepots. This was actually done at the request of a site owner, but there is no reason a landscape architect couldn't also encourage the use of alternative products by working with growers willing to use them. As above, this is especially true when the designer has significant control over the installation of a project, either because he or she is a design-build professional or the project is a private landscape and the designer will be heavily involved in selection of all project elements. As with several items on this checklist, designers and owners may not be able to change practices immediately, but they can use leverage as a specifier and recommender to encourage changes to standard practices in the future. In all cases, owners and landscape architects should make it clear they will continue to work with green industry professionals willing to embrace improved environmental practices over time. This will show there is profit to be made from such initiatives.

Changing internal practices

❏ **Reuse plant pots.** Nursery practices vary considerably as to whether plant pots are reused as is (which can raise concerns about disease), steamed to remove pathogens, or simply tossed. Whenever possible, nurseries should consider reusing their pots. The time and money invested in cleaning, steaming, and sorting used pots could be recaptured by not having to buy as many new pots.

❏ **Actively recycle plant pots.** Both growers and installers should, without fail, participate in any recycling programs that exist in their regions. Barring an established recycling program, growers, nurseries, and garden centers could consider creating their own, likely in collaboration with their local professional organization. The trips that customers and installers make to a plant seller's facility could translate into additional purchases.

❏ **Consider renewable materials.** There are several ways green industry professionals can begin to introduce alternative pot materials. Growers could start plants in manure pots rather than peat or plastic. They could seek out plastic pots that are made from recycled plastic, like those from East Jordan Plastics in Michigan. Installers and managers (including owners) could consider manure, peat, plant fiber, or paper pots, especially for annuals or native plugs, which are typically installed at a small size. Growers could offer environmentally sound options like paper or plant fiber, then promote those products to owners and installers.

Advocacy

- **Learn about local recycling programs and spread the word.** It is not unusual for landscape architects and green industry professionals to be asked landscape-related questions at parties or playdates ("what do I do with my sick tree?" being perhaps the most common). Many consumers of garden-center plants end up with lots of plastic pots they don't know how to dispose of. Landscape installers, managers, and designers should be ready for this inevitable question with specifics on where those pots can be taken for recycling. Similarly, local American Society of Landscape Architects (ASLA), Professional Landscape Design Association, and green industry chapters should publicize any recycling days, programs, or efforts to other landscape professionals and the general public.

- **Establish a recycling program.** True, that's a taller order than telling friends where to recycle, but there is at least one good model to follow (see the case study in this chapter). Establishing a program will likely take the attention of a local ASLA chapter or a local green industry chapter; they may even need to work together. It will be important to consider all phases of the waste stream: how the pots are collected, how they are transported to a recycling facility, and what recycling facility will accept them. All these items need to be in place, as the MNLA has learned over the years, in order to create an effective regionwide program. Local volunteers might participate in a designated collect-sort-and-wash weekend, where dirty pots are prepared for recycling, eliminating the extra time and trouble for consumers and contractors. Volunteers could also drive trucks to transport the pots to a recycling facility.

- **Add recycling requirements to standard specifications.** Landscape architects in public practice often have responsibility both for overseeing the design and construction of individual projects and for updating any standard specifications or contract terms their agencies use. State departments of transportation usually have voluminous standard specifications, while other federal, state, and local units of government may require certain things in every construction contract, like prevailing wages, limited plant lists, and payment policies. Landscape architects in the public realm could work to require plastic pot recycling as a requirement of all contracts written through their agencies. There should, of course, be a local recycling program in place or a willing recycler in the area, but, given those, making recycling a standard practice levels the playing field on public bids and would immediately keep a renewable resource from local landfills.

CASE STUDY: MINNESOTA NURSERY AND LANDSCAPE ASSOCIATION

Plastic pot recycling seems to be getting done primarily because it's the right thing to do. There's very little profit in it, and many nurseries, industry organizations, and contractors have found it more trouble than it's worth. The MNLA has implemented one of the largest programs in the nation, built on the cooperation and (to some degree) altruism of participating collection points. "They do it because they feel they should do it," says Jon Horsman, the MNLA program's manager. "There's a desire to be part of an industry that can truly make a claim of being an environmental industry. We have to take responsibility for our waste and our products."

The MNLA program began in 2006. Ten suppliers—companies that were selling plants primarily to landscape contractors—collected pots on two designated weekends, and the pots were recycled by a local waste collection company. The program collected fifty tons of plastic that first year, which Horsman said wasn't an amazing number, but it was enough to tell them "there was something there; that we should move forward." Unfortunately, the MNLA had to find a new recycler in 2007 because the first was no longer interested. Then the organization needed another in 2010, after the second recycler went belly-up.

Today, the MNLA works with forty-five garden centers and six plant suppliers to collect pots from both contractors and consumers and transport them to Choice Plastics, a Twin Cities company that specializes in recycling (as its name suggests) plastics. Choice has been huge for the program, according to Horsman, and it even collected recycling pots from previous years that were never actually recycled. Choice's particular expertise at finding markets for the after-market plastic has made the program a worthwhile venture. Choice gets used plastic delivered to its door for free, and it gets to sell it on the back end. Add in processing costs, though, and profit margins are small. Says Horsman, "They're not building their business around [our program]."

The MNLA program now collects all summer from across the central part of Minnesota. About three dozen garden centers and suppliers have permanent collection bins, while the rest still participate in collection events one weekend in June and one in September. The collectors bear all the costs of cleaning, sorting, and delivering to Choice Plastics. In 2010 the program collected two million pounds—a twenty-fold increase since the program's inception.

The key to the MNLA program has been to address, with key partners, each step of the recycling process. The MNLA has established collection points (the garden centers and suppliers), determined who will recycle the materials (Choice Plastics), and planned for transportation to the recycler (by asking the collectors to bear that cost). The MNLA itself handles the publicity by listing collectors on its website and heavily promoting the two major collection weekends. Though new programs in other regions could operate differently, they must also consider this entire recycling process in order to be effective.

3: Vehicle Fuel: An Addiction to Oil

Among the most maligned of summer sounds is the drone of the backpack leaf blower. Among the worst summer smells is the acrid emissions of a groaning skidsteer. And among the most ominous of summer sights is the bulk of a diesel mini dump truck parked, trailer in tow, at the side of a residential street, idling. Each of these sensory assaults means one thing: the use of fossil fuels to install or take care of landscapes.

This is unavoidable. Without trucks, excavators, skidsteers, compactors, mowers, trimmers, and blowers, landscape work would reel back to the last century, when armies of laborers chopped at the earth for years to make railroads, cities, and parks. Today, that method would be considered far too slow and far too expensive. The fact is, though, that vehicle emissions are the most significant single contributor to global climate change—and for vehicle fuel we need to consider not only the fuel actually used in the landscaping machines, but also the environmental cost of oil extraction, the fuel it takes to transport the fuel (often from halfway around the world), the energy it takes to refine the raw crude, and the fuel it takes to bring the fuel to the gas station.

The creation and management of landscapes requires fuel in four primary ways, each with its own issues and solutions. Nurseries use trucks and small runabouts within their facilities to move plants and materials around, so that managers and staff can visit various greenhouses and growing yards quickly and efficiently. In many cases, growing yards can be vast, and one company may have different yards miles apart, necessitating travel by vehicle.

Landscape contractors use trucks and trailers to transport plants, materials, and equipment to a job site. At the smallest scale is the ubiquitous small flatbed or dump truck filled with plants, rocks, and mulch, with a hitch for a skidsteer trailer. At the largest scale are semitrucks pulling flatbeds with major excavation equipment or side dumpers filled with soil and rock. Once on the jobsite, the skidsteers whirl and scoop, the excavators lock down and dig away, and the front loaders and cranes move and place rocks and gravel. From large sites to small, the sound of a landscape being installed is a chorus of back-up beeps and the constant groan of internal combustion.

Once a project is finished, and on into perpetuity, management companies visit with mowers, leaf blowers, and motorized trimmers to maintain the landscape. The equipment arrives on trailers behind trucks, zooms about for a few hours, then leaves on those same trucks with trailers. Though it is impossible to quantify what a typical landscape costs in fuel (in part because there is no typical landscape project), suffice it to say that these machines are built for power and convenience, not efficiency.

Federal regulations and new equipment

Equipment used for landscape construction and maintenance is regulated under two different Environmental Protection Agency (EPA) programs. Anything under 25 horsepower and not diesel powered is considered a small-spark-ignition (small SI) engine. That includes most riding and push mowers and anything handheld: blowers, trimmers, saws, and so on. The big ones—skidsteers, excavators, and graders—are considered "nonroad diesel engines." In both cases, the EPA regulates emissions, not efficiency, with rules on hydrocarbons (HC), nitrogen oxides (NOx), carbon monoxide (CO), and particulate matter (PM). (The first two of these appear together on most regulations as HC+NOx.)[1]

In 2007 significant new regulations came into effect for almost all nonroad engines. In that year, new emissions rules for nonroad diesel engines began to be phased in with the groundbreaking nationwide requirement for low-sulfur diesel fuel. Previously unregulated sulfur quantities were reduced to an allowed 500 parts per million in 2007 (the same requirement as for highway diesel). Nonroad diesel requirements dropped again to a maximum 15 parts per million in 2010. This so-called ultra-low sulfur fuel was necessary for equipment manufacturers to implement emissions control technology on their vehicles; that technology can be damaged by sulfur. (This fuel-first, vehicles-second regulation tactic is similar to the process for reducing car emissions in the 1970s, when leaded fuel was phased out to protect emissions-reducing catalytic converters.) On the heels of the new fuel requirements, new particulate matter and NOx emissions rules became law in 2008 for diesel engines less than 25 horsepower, while all nonroad diesel engines will see significant improvement between 2011 and 2015, depending on the engine size.

The main thing to remember here is that the EPA has rolled out new requirements since 1996 in stringency levels called "tiers." Tier 3 is the law of the land right now. The final standards are Tier 4, but there is an Interim Tier 4 that is mostly in place now. Interim Tier 4 is better than Tier 3, and Tier 4 is better than Interim Tier 4. Without getting into the specific numbers, suffice it to say that the difference between Tier 3 and Interim Tier 4 is absolutely huge: around a 90 percent reduction in allowable particulate matter and a 50 percent reduction in NOx. Tier 4 further reduces NOx about another 80 percent. These are important steps in curbing emissions for landscape equipment. Most skidsteers and mini excavators come in under 100 horsepower, putting them in either the 25 to 75 horsepower category or the 75 to 175 horsepower category, both of which must meet Final Tier 4 standards by 2013. Anything under 25 horsepower must already comply with Tier 4. Most manufacturers publish their tier compliance prominently in their equipment specifications, suggesting they are competing to get ahead of the game and win customers by complying early.[2]

In 2007 the EPA also completed its full phase-in of emissions standards for handheld small SI engines that began to be implemented in 2000. Significant reductions are required under this so-called Phase 2 rule. In 2002, leaf blowers and trimmers were allowed around 200 grams per kilowatt hour (g/kW-hr) of combined hydrocarbon and nitrous oxide (HC+NOx) emission. In model year 2007 and beyond, that allowance is down to 50 g/kW-hr. That means a 2007 leaf blower is four times cleaner than a 2002 leaf blower. Non-handheld small SI engines, found in most lawn mowers, were required to meet fleetwide improvement by 2005, but a 2008 rule requires even greater improvement in model years 2011 (for a group of engine types generally including lawn and garden tractors) and 2012 (for a group generally comprising walk-behind mowers).

Because all landscape installation and maintenance equipment has gained fairly recent emissions regulations, the best way to gain efficiency and reduce pollution is for installers, nurseries, and management companies to replace their fleets. This can also increase fuel efficiency. The new small engine standards, for instance, have forced manufacturers to modify the way fuel moves through a small engine. Where some fuel used to blow past the typical two-stroke design, now much more of it is used by the engine. This means that unburned fuel is not simply jettisoned into the landscape as it once was. That is both cleaner and saves fuel. That gassy mower smell will eventually be a thing of the past, but not until landscapers replace their fleets, like Pacific Landscape Management has done (see the case study in this chapter).

Though fleet replacement seems a costly proposition, there is inherent efficiency in these better engines. Pacific is saving 15,000 gallons of fuel per year (more than $50,000 at $3.50 per gallon) and has made back its investment in two years.

Put simply, hand-held equipment should be model year 2007 or newer, nondiesel tractors and mowers should be 2011 or newer, and walk-behind mowers should be 2012 or newer. In addition, landscapers should be planning to replace their skidsteers, mini excavators, and other construction equipment in 2013.

Right-sizing

The sentiment that "you don't kill a fly with a sledgehammer" could apply to vehicle use in the green industry. No installer would bring a road grader to level down a small patch of lawn, of course, but there are other places where "right-sizing" could bring environmental benefit and cost savings. And sometimes the right-size equipment doesn't use fuel at all.

One Green World in Oregon uses bicycles equipped with storage baskets, and now most trips across the grounds are done under human power. The bicycles are just the right size for a trip to a work area if only a little bit of equipment is needed (a pruner, some tools, etc.). Pacific's project managers go into the field in Toyota Priuses rather than in pick-up tricks. The thinking is that when a manager goes to check in with a crew managing a landscape, he or she doesn't need the same pick-up truck with excellent towing ability that the crew itself does. Those visits are about inspection and communication, so they can be done in a car, in this case one of the most fuel-efficient cars on the market.

One of the main uses of the Rancho Verde development in Chicago (see the first case study in chapter 4) is to provide a staging ground for landscape installers from outside the city. Rather than running their large trucks, often half-filled, from suburban home bases to every in-town job site, these companies can rent space and bring larger quantities of materials to Rancho Verde on larger trucks with fewer trips. Then, as needed, the materials can go to local job sites on smaller, more efficient trucks. The companies can then right-size their deliveries by making sure every truck trip is full of materials.

Conservation

American Green, Ted Steinberg's excellent and frightening examination of lawn care, says that Americans spill about 17 million gallons of fuel on the ground simply from refilling their lawn mowers. That, Steinberg reminds us, is 50 percent more oil than was spilled from the Exxon *Valdez*.[3] Landscapers have the same problem. It is infamously easy to spill gasoline when using a small plastic tank to fill a small gas reservoir like those on blowers and mowers. Though the commercial filling stations most landscapers have at their facilities are required by law to have shut-off nozzles, the cans they take into the field are not. Pacific Landscape Management in Oregon replaced all its portable gas tanks with spill-preventing ones, of the brand No-Spill.[4] These cans release gasoline at the push of a button on the nozzle, to prevent spillage before the nozzle is in the mower tank. The nozzle also shuts off when gas backs up into it (like a commercial nozzle), signaling that the receiving tank is full. These cans are a simple and inexpensive solution that protects the environment and can save a contractor fuel and money.

Fuel can also be conserved at larger nurseries through the nursery design itself. Midwest Groundcovers is divided into four growing areas, each of which operates almost like a separate nursery. Crews tend to work within a single area, moving around a 30-acre site rather than the full 120 acres. This has effectively cut vehicle miles in half, by reducing the distance of all trips.

CHECKLIST

Creating plans and specifications

❑ **Include a no-idling rule.** Different landscape contractors have different perspectives on fuel use. Some are already very conscientious about turning vehicles off when they are not in use; others prefer to keep them running curbside. The fact is that there is little reason to keep a vehicle's engine on while it is being loaded or unloaded, or while a construction company employee visits the construction trailer. Typical plans and specifications do set forth general conditions for contractors, which may include prevailing wage rules, policies related to the condition of the site overnight, and designated staging areas for construction vehicles and materials. Owners and landscape architects could add to this section a policy that forbids the idling of vehicles when they are not in active use. True, this may be difficult for an owner's representative to monitor, but if there is a full-time site inspector, provided by either the owner or a design firm, writing this policy into the specification makes it an enforceable rule, rather than an occasional suggestion. The benefit to the contractor, of course, is that the company will use less fuel and therefore save money. The Sustainable Sites Initiative (see chapter 7) has recognized this as an attainable goal and offers certification points for implementing such a policy.

❑ **Require spill-reducing filling systems for on-site refueling.** If installation or maintenance equipment is to be filled on a project site, plans and specifications can require that filling be done in specific locations and in certain ways. The best way of reducing fuel spillage and waste on a project site (and thereby to also keep the site healthier) is to require some type of spill-preventing gas can.

❑ **Require EPA emissions compliance.** Yes, all construction equipment manufactured today must meet current EPA standards, but there is plenty of old equipment out there. There can be a major difference between model years, as described in this chapter. Though it would be an aggressive move, owners and landscape architects could decide to require compliance with the most current EPA rule. The Sustainable Sites Initiative gives points for this practice, and it is theoretically possible that it could be written into project and standard specifications, in the interest of managing the air quality at the project site.

Working with green industry professionals

❑ **Choose or recommend installers and management companies with environmental credibility.** As described in the plant pot checklist, many installers and maintenance companies rely on recommendations from designers and owners for a portion of their business. Those recommendations should therefore be reserved for companies working to reduce their fuel consumption. One key way to verify this is to ask how new maintenance equipment is and to ask about the efficiency of installation equipment. Designers and owners could also ask about any other fuel-saving initiatives, like the use of biodiesel or hybrid trucks. Fuel management should be one facet of making a recommendation based on environmental performance (see "Questions for installers" and "Questions for management companies" in chapter 8).

❑ **Work with growers who are reducing their fuel use.** On jobs where landscape architects have some say over the selection of a grower—like those where plants are custom grown or when the designer is also the installer—designers should consider the fuel use of growers. One Green World and Midwest Groundcovers have demonstrated that there are many ways to reduce fuel use (bicycling within the site, biodiesel tractors, site layout), and designers should ask about similar initiatives that growers are taking on. Similarly, owners that work directly with growers on projects such as native landscape restorations or annual flower plantings could consider fuel use when selecting growers. In discussions like these, owners and landscape architects should always stress the potential cost savings of reducing fuel use on a nursery site.

❏ **Consider where installers and management companies are located.** When owners select green industry professionals for ongoing contracts, they should consider how far the installer or maintainer must travel to get to the project site. Owners can have a hand in significantly reducing vehicle miles by working with contractors that are in closer proximity to their sites. This is especially true for management companies. Pacific concentrates its business in the western suburbs of Portland; Lambert Landscape Company, based in Dallas, only maintains landscapes within a five- to six-mile radius of its office. As competition increases among management companies for more scarce work, they will be willing to go farther afield to find jobs, with the prospect of increased fuel use.

Changing internal practices

❏ **Evaluate transportation within a nursery site.** Nurseries vary widely in scale, so it would be disingenuous to recommend a specific solution for all growing facilities. Though One Green World uses bicycles on its site, it is rather small, compared to a company like Midwest Groundcovers or any other major grower. However, nurseries should consider carefully the environmental impact of how employees travel around their sites. They should think about hybrid vehicles, nonmotorized vehicles, biodiesel vehicles, and any other option that would reduce fossil fuel use. The benefit to the environment is obvious, but such a change will likely also save a nursery money.

❏ **Switch to spill-reducing gas cans.** Changing out all in-field fueling cans to ones that help prevent spills is a simple, inexpensive solution. Nurseries, installers, landscape management companies, and owners with their own maintenance divisions all fuel on-site—that is, away from regulated fueling stations. Such organizations could save money and reduce environmental impact with this simple change.

❏ **Institute a no idling policy.** Though recent high fuel prices have made turning off a vehicle when not in use much more common, many installers and management companies still idle trucks, mowers, and construction equipment. It is in the best interest of these companies to establish and enforce a no idling policy. This initiative would cost nothing and would begin saving the company money immediately, as well as, of course, reducing fossil fuel use.

❏ **Upgrade out-of-date equipment.** When Pacific Landscape Management upgraded its fleet of mowers, blowers, and trimmers, it saw dividends almost immediately. Because of the significant recent and forthcoming changes in federal regulation, now is the perfect time to upgrade, because new machines will be clearly more efficient than ones even a few years old. Yes, this will take some capital investment, but parks departments, campuses, and installation and maintenance companies that do this will likely see a short-term payback.

Advocacy

❑ **Support increased fuel efficiency and reduced emissions.** Periodically the EPA, on direction from Congress, updates standards for cars, trucks, and small engines. This is often a contentious debate, with advocates citing the need for cleaner air and less dependence on foreign oil, and opponents claiming impacts to business success and job creation. Because such regulations have no effect on equipment and vehicles currently in the field, owners, designers, and the green industry should support them as a means of improving future performance as landscape contractors and management companies upgrade their equipment over time. Pacific Landscape Management actually saw a very short-term return on investment when it voluntarily upgraded its fleet in 2008 and 2009.

This indicates that upgrades to equipment with improved efficiency will also save installers and maintainers money. When these policy changes or bills are announced, landscape architects, site managers, the ASLA, and other professional organizations, both local and national, should lobby and advocate for their acceptance, as an investment in healthier landscapes in the future.

❑ **Incentivize equipment upgrades.** Many landscape architects and owners have relationships with preferred installation and maintenance professionals. These close relationships, which are often very beneficial to the installer or maintainer, could be leveraged to assist the green industry company in phasing out older small engines. The recent EPA rules were a turning point for the green industry, because all new small engines—landscape workhorses like mowers, blowers, and trimmers—are significantly improved over previous models. Owners and landscape architects could work with their preferred companies to phase out old equipment, perhaps even by helping finance new equipment, which the contractor can pay back over time with money saved on fuel. This is an aggressive proposal, but older small engines are profoundly inefficient and polluting, and eliminating them from the landscape would save fuel and clean the air.

CASE STUDY:
PACIFIC LANDSCAPE MANAGEMENT

Pacific Landscape Management primarily maintains landscapes. It has been in business since 2001 and takes care of about six hundred acres of mostly corporate campuses and commercial properties in the western suburbs of Portland, Oregon. In 2008 Bob Grover, Pacific's president, began to push environmental efforts, in large part because he started hearing from his clients. He noticed that commercial owners were asking more and more about Pacific's environmental performance, and Grover saw the writing on the wall: the company could lose business if it couldn't satisfactorily answer clients' environmental questions, or, inversely, it could win business by marketing its environmental practices. It was only later that the company discovered it could save itself and clients a lot of money by going green.

Take vehicle fuel, for instance. In 2008 and 2009, Pacific replaced its entire small engine fleet: 150 pieces of equipment. With this upgrade, the company retired its old dirty two-stroke engines and bought equipment that meets current EPA standards. The replacement was a significant investment, but the company saved 15,000 gallons of fuel in the first year and saw a return on investment within just two years. Today, Pacific is spending around $50,000 less per year on fuel than it used to, and the machines are paid off. The fuel savings is the equivalent of 180 fewer passenger cars on the road per year. The workhorse now is the Stihl four-mix engine, which, according to Grover's research, has the lowest emissions on the market.

The company is also saving fuel with No-Spill gas cans, and Pacific managers now drive Toyota Priuses, rather than big pick-up trucks, to visit job sites.

Pacific is also experimenting with its own landscape, which has the added benefit of showing off green landscape ideas to potential clients who visit the site. A linear rain garden runs between the parking lot and the front of the building, and this garden manages about half the roof's runoff. A variety of drought-tolerant groundcover plantings carpet the boulevard between street and sidewalk, in test plots meant to simulate the harsh conditions in parking-lot islands. Based on this experiment, Pacific has convinced at least one client to replace poorly performing and resource-intensive turf in its islands. In an adjacent mini-storage company's front lawn between the sidewalk and the road, Pacific installed and is maintaining a fescue-only lawn and an eco-lawn, which includes various cold- and warm-season grasses, as well as clover. The company has a vertical wall set up for testing plants—everything from traditional green-roof plants to unexpected ones like *Bergenia* and miniature conifers. And Pacific delivers all its job-site green waste to a local composting facility.

Pacific used federal and state tax credits to install photovoltaic panels on its warehouse roof, and the panels now generate 90 percent of the company's electricity needs. The return on investment was achieved in a modest five years. Grover stresses, however, that the big savings on energy have come from just being conscientious. The incremental change of turning off lights, leaving doors open for breezes, and keeping the air conditioning off more often has resulted in a 20 percent annual energy savings compared to before these practices were implemented.

Grover says Pacific has also been experimenting with organic fertilizers, and it has settled on a mix of 40 percent organic and 60 percent synthetic, by volume, which the company calls Pacific Landscape Organic Blend. Though it's not all the way to organic (something Grover doesn't feel is effective enough), that change has eliminated the use of thirty tons of synthetic fertilizer since 2008.

Grover's biggest green push, though, is irrigation. He's a big believer in weather-based irrigation, and he tries to convince every client to switch to a Rain Bird ET Manager (his favorite product). A weather-based system gets continuous updates from regional weather stations, so a computer can decide when and how much to water. The cheapest water is rainwater, and though most irrigation systems come with rain sensors (hopefully the days of watering in the rain are over), Grover feels that's not smart enough. A weather-based system can weigh factors like on-site evapotranspiration data and real-time weather data to alter or override standard control programs. This helps conserve water when, say, rain is on the way or when conditions are dry but actual water loss is minimal.[5]

The Rain Bird system requires greater up-front cost and a periodic subscription to the weather service, but the cost savings from reduced water use offsets those expenditures, according to Grover. Pacific has installed more than 150 of these systems, and the water savings typically brings the return on investment down to two years. (Other major irrigation companies have ET systems—the ET stands for evapotranspiration—that focus on data gathered on-site.) Those 150 clients amount to a water savings of 54 million gallons, or the equivalent of 400 households, every year. One major client, the AmberGlen Corporate Center, a 217-acre campus just west of Portland, saw a 40 percent reduction in water use for irrigation, with no effect on plant material.

Of course, many of the things Pacific is doing—from weather-based irrigation to lawn alternatives—have to be sold to a client, typically a bottom-line-driven client who wants everything to look great at minimal expense. So Pacific has created a slideshow that lays out the empirical data on the cost savings of a variety of environmentally friendly practices, the suggestion being that Pacific can pass along some of those savings to the client. Grover is competing with tiny companies with a pick-up truck and a few mowers, so he has an uphill battle to win clients anyway, even without having to convince them that his environmental practices won't cost more in the long run. He's managing it, though, which is nice for the region, and also a lesson for other management companies, owners, and designers.

4: Energy Consumption: Power to the Plants

All that plants need to grow is reliable sun and a little water, right? Not quite. Baby plants must be coddled to maturity. They must be provided optimum growing conditions, including just the right temperature and sun exposure (see more on water needs in chapter 5). That typically means they are started as seedlings in greenhouses. True, a greenhouse is designed to capture the sun's energy and amplify it, to create a warmer environment inside than out, but the fact is that greenhouses are usually heated, especially at nurseries in colder northern climates. The inside of a greenhouse is a vast space, typically with thin plastic walls, and it requires a significant input of heat to maintain a constant temperature.

Offices, too, require energy, for lighting, heating, and cooling. That is true, of course, of all buildings, but the offices of growers, landscape contractors, and maintenance companies are often combined with massive equipment garages in large warehouse-like buildings. Also, due to the indoor-to-outdoor nature of the business, office doors are constantly opening and closing as staff move about the facility. This permeability of the building envelope reduces energy efficiency and costs money.

High-performance buildings and alternative energy

Building technology has advanced significantly in the last few decades. Smart buildings sense and redistribute the interior air of different temperatures to regulate climate without as much actual heating and cooling. Architectural details allow sun in when it's needed for heating and provide shade when it would be too hot. Tight envelopes and high-tech windows prevent heat gain and loss through the building's skin. These technologies come at a premium, of course, and are best built into new buildings rather than retrofitted onto existing warehouses. That's why high-performance green industry buildings like Christy Webber's in Chicago are rare (see the case study in this chapter). That company's offices are separated from the equipment garage and placed in a sleek steel structure with all the best bells and whistles. Christy Webber Landscapes (CWL) estimates that its building consumes about half the electricity of a comparable building.[1]

Nurseries, however, stand in a unique position because many of their buildings are effectively replaced every few years. The typical greenhouse is a Quonset hut with a plastic roof, but that plastic gets battered and needs to be replaced occasionally. One Green World (see the case study in chapter 1) uses double layers of plastic with an air pocket in between for insulation. It looks like a typical greenhouse but maintains interior heat more effectively. One Green World has also taken a page from permanent building efficiencies in its greenhouses by installing radiant heating.

Though it hasn't been explored widely, the green industry could easily consider geothermal and solar systems. Generally, these companies have plenty of land and plenty of sun access—both requirements for large growing fields or equipment-staging areas, but also ideal for alternative energy generation. Pacific Landscape Management has solar electric panels on its roof (see the case study in chapter 3). CWL has geothermal wells under an outdoor employee–use plaza and solar thermal panels on its building roof.

Another possible option would be to use the greenhouses for heating. Built into the top floor of the CWL Chicago building is an enclosed room originally meant for experimentation with plants. It has south-facing windows and, year-round, the room gets significantly hotter than the rest of the building. The smart ventilation system in the building is able to draw air from this interior greenhouse and distribute it throughout the building in winter in order to reduce heating costs.

Geothermal heating and cooling setups essentially use the constant temperature from underground to provide a boost to heating systems in winter and cooling systems in summer. The ground stays at between 50 and 60 degrees year-round, depending on a site's latitude. A geothermal system includes water- or antifreeze-filled pipes that descend into the earth, where the liquid ends up at the same temperature as the ground. In winter, a heat pump inside the building concentrates the heat in the 50- to 60-degree water (warmer than the outdoor air) and distributes that heat through the building. In the summer, because the 50- to 60-degree water is cooler than the exterior air, the heat pump can work in reverse, pulling heat out of a building and into the water. More typical forced air systems use electricity or fossil fuel to create either heat (with the furnace flame) or cooling (with the air conditioner's condenser). In a geothermal system the heat and cooling comes from the constant temperature in the ground and electricity powers only the heat pump. The head start provided by the constant ground temperature makes geothermal systems around twice as efficient as conventional systems.[2]

Geothermal systems are initially more expensive than conventional forced air systems, but the cost continues to come down and the energy cost savings over time are significant. In some cases, companies can break even on their investment in as little as five years. The most efficient geothermal systems require plenty of space for multiple vertical pipes, and those pipes should ideally be located near the building to be heated, to prevent temperature loss between the ground and the heat pump. This fact makes them somewhat problematic in dense urban environments. Nurseries and landscape installation and management companies, however, almost always have ample space. Someday, growers may be able to heat greenhouses with geothermally boosted radiant systems, or systems could be installed under adjacent equipment-staging and fueling areas in order to heat and cool office buildings.

Incremental change

Through the years, politicians have been mocked for asking the nation to solve climate change by turning lights off and turning down the air conditioning a few degrees. These, however, are important projects and ones that are notoriously hard to implement in a business environment. However, the inherent indoor-to-outdoor nature of the green industry provides an excellent opportunity for these companies to implement incremental changes that could reduce companies' energy consumption and save them money. For a break from a 90- or 95-degree day in the field, entering a building cooled to 75 degrees instead of the more typical 72 or even 68 will seem downright pleasant. Pacific Landscape Management has realized a 20 percent savings in energy costs over the last few years simply by making sure lights are turned off and by keeping the air conditioning off more often.

One Green World attached plastic gaskets around all its greenhouse doors to prevent warm air from escaping between the door and its frame—one of the most permeable points of a greenhouse, also typically located right underneath the heat fans. Incremental change could also include motion sensors for office and conference room lights, focused work lights in equipment warehouses rather than large banks of overhead fluorescents, a computer-off policy at night, and compact fluorescent lighting.

CHECKLIST

Of the five areas of environmental improvement within the green industry, landscape architects and owners can have the least effect on energy consumption. Most of the improvements in energy use will take place within those companies' actual facilities, over which clients have little say. However, as discussed in the checklists for the previous two chapters, owners and landscape architects can use the power of recommendations to work with green industry companies in order to make changes.

A key point: it is neither fair nor effective to simply withhold recommendations (or contracts) from green industry companies based on their current performance. Landscape architects and owners should work with vendors over time, always suggesting improvements, always making it clear that

such initiatives will solidify future recommendations. There are companies already succeeding in reducing their energy consumption, but unless new companies also make those efforts, overall environmental improvement in the industry will stall.

Chapter 8 includes several lists of questions that can be asked of green industry companies to begin to determine a company's overall environmental credibility.

Changing internal practices
❑ **Perform an energy audit and then make incremental changes.** Because of the indoor-to-outdoor nature of many nurseries and landscape businesses—and also because many of these companies have facilities that have expanded organically over time with business needs—such companies may not have an accurate handle on their actual energy consumption. Change cannot take place without accurate data. Green industry professionals can hire outside consultants to perform energy audits, or they can do the research themselves. In either case, this audit should form the basis for making incremental changes, like computer and electricity use policies, thermostat adjustments, and replacement of inefficient lighting and appliances.

❑ **Install an alternative-energy generation system.** Because of the amount of open land they typically occupy, nurseries and landscape installation and management companies often have the space and sun access to truly benefit from geothermal, solar thermal, and solar electric systems. These can come with significant investment, but there may be local or federal tax credits available. A geothermal system, in particular, which can be installed under a parking lot or equipment-staging area, is becoming highly cost competitive. Green industry companies should consider this option, particularly when they are faced with replacing a heating or cooling system.

❑ **Improve greenhouse efficiency.** Most growers heat their greenhouses. Most greenhouses have walls of single-ply plastic, which could be upgraded the next time the plastic sheathing is replaced. Growers should also consider better gasketing around greenhouse entrances and radiant heating to replace or augment the more typical over-door blowers.

❑ **View expansion or relocation as an opportunity to improve energy efficiency.** It is generally more expensive to retrofit an existing building for prime energy efficiency than to add the latest technology to a new building. Green industry companies don't move all that often, but when they do, they should consider the cost and the environmental and marketing benefits of creating a new highly efficient building, as a showcase of their environmental commitment.

Beneath the employee plaza at Christy Webber Landscapes is a geothermal system, and a solar well preheats the air entering the maintenance shop. (Christy Webber Landscapes)

CASE STUDY: CHRISTY WEBBER LANDSCAPES

The entrance to the Christy Webber Landscapes headquarters features solar thermal panels.

Christy Webber has been in the green industry since 1988, when she began mowing lawns in Chicago neighborhoods. She started her eponymous firm in 1990 and has built it into a major landscape design, installation, and maintenance company that employs around 250 people. That company is, at its corporate headquarters on Chicago's west side, trying to provide an alternative to the typical landscaper's corporate headquarters. Christy Webber Landscapes (CWL) is the developer and main tenant of Rancho Verde, a nursery industry incubator on a former brownfield site. It's immediately adjacent to the Chicago Center for Green Technology and sports bioswales and permeable paving.

In the early 2000s, as the company was contemplating expansion, the City of Chicago was marketing a roughly thirty-acre site sandwiched between commuter rail tracks and historic parkways and a short distance from the Garfield Park Conservatory and the elevated green line. The mayor's office had been envisioning the near west side as "green town" (a moniker in keeping with Chicago's other neighborhoods, like Boystown, Greektown, Wrigleyville, etc.). Webber hired the landscape architecture firm Hitchcock Design Group to create a master plan that would wow the city enough to sell the land to them—hopefully at a discount.

That's exactly what happened. Chicago cleaned up the site (it was formerly an industrial wasteyard) and sold the whole parcel to CWL for a bargain price. Rancho Verde wraps

A green roof and greenhouse atop Christy Webber Landscapes's building help lower energy consumption for heating and cooling. (Christy Webber Landscapes)

around the Chicago Center for Green Technology and another site used by Greencorps Chicago, a city initiative that trains disadvantaged populations in landscaping and horticulture methods, then deploys them throughout the city to maintain its green spaces. Webber uses twelve acres, and the rest is composed of staging lots for five other landscaping companies.

In the middle of the site is a permeable concrete paver public street that ends with a cul-de-sac around a large rain garden. CWL's LEED Platinum building, designed by Doug Farr, sits right on the street, and the staging areas and utility buildings are just behind. All the water on CWL's site drains to storm-water swales, though the company doesn't reuse any of it. However, there is a 32,000-gallon cistern that collects rain from the maintenance building roof for watering plants.

The most visible attempts at environmental sustainability at CWL are associated with the buildings, rather than with the landscape. The office building, a sexy raw steel shed, uses solar thermal and geothermal sources to completely eliminate gas heating and cooling. An active climate control system searches for cooler or warmer parts of the building, then draws air in from those areas, so intake air is closer to the temperature of the fresh air, reducing energy needs. This process is helped by a rooftop greenhouse, which is always warm. (The greenhouse, says Webber, is really a showpiece and is used only for vegetable cultivation by employees.) The office building also has a green roof, and the maintenance facility uses a vertical solar well, which preheats air for winter warmth.

The most important feature of Rancho Verde, though, is its location. Most landscape companies, by spatial necessity, have to be based outside the city. This increases cost and fuel consumption for every inner-city project. Rancho Verde brings landscape companies (not just CWL) closer to their projects. The other tenants use it as staging grounds by bringing big truckloads of plants in periodically, then using smaller trucks to serve jobsites. That's far more cost-effective and more fuel-efficient than having those small trucks drive all the way in from the suburbs to each job site.

But while CWL has made strides in changing its on-site landscape practices, Webber bemoans her inability to extend that out to the jobsite. CWL's business manager, Roger Post, believes the company might be able to market a "green crew" for environmentally minded clients with a little extra to spend, but he admits the big money is in public jobs, which come with competitive bids. "Everybody wants to be green," says Webber, "but nobody wants to pay for it." In fact, she worries about the current perception that CWL is more expensive than their competitors, a perception that arises exactly because of their facilities and green practices. CWL still wins public bids, however, in essence proving that the company's greening hasn't affected its ability to keep costs competitive.

CASE STUDY: OREGON ASSOCIATION OF NURSERIES

The Oregon Association of Nurseries (OAN) represents more than one thousand nurseries in the third largest nursery-production state in the nation (after California and Florida). Oregon is known for being a shade greener (environmentally speaking) than most places, but nursery practices have, until recently, remained business as usual. Then, a few years ago, some OAN board members began to see environmental practices as a way to benefit member businesses. This was because, according to Whitney Rideout, OAN's business development manager, the OAN did a market study that proved that design professionals were getting more requests from consumers for environmentally sound plants.

Based on those board members' perspectives, the OAN sought and won a grant from the Oregon Department of Agriculture to implement a variety of new initiatives. That funding was later complemented by more money from the Northwest Energy Efficiency Alliance. Though Rideout cautions that the OAN is only two years into its program, the organization has begun to generate data and change practices. The data gathering itself is no small feat; on its own it would make these programs worthwhile, because good data are generally lacking in the green industry.

One initiative that is well underway is the Climate Friendly Nurseries Project (CFNP). The main goal of this program is the reduction of greenhouse gases, primarily through improved energy efficiency. Though the project's final findings won't be available until 2013, the OAN published interim guides in 2010 and 2011 that document best practices for nurseries. Each practice—like retrofitting lighting, steam-cleaning pots and soil, and installing better greenhouse covers—is applied to two theoretical nurseries, one that is forty acres in size and one that is four hundred acres. Tables in the guides show costs, savings, and the payback timeline as well as case studies (including one on One Green World) of nurseries that have implemented the practices. Though clearly geared toward the nursery industry and limited to users in Oregon, the guides could be useful to design professionals and owners wanting to gain an understanding of the implications of environmental practices on their green industry partners, as well as to green industry professionals interested in implementing similar improvements in other parts of the country. The guides are available online (see Notes and Resources).

Another OAN initiative dealing with energy is the "25 percent in 10 years" energy pilot program. Rideout explains that nurseries, many of which have grown over time and added facilities as they were needed, often have a bevy of electricity and gas meters without really knowing what they track. The energy pilot program is a voluntary commitment by the OAN to, as its name suggests, reduce industrywide energy use by 25 percent in ten years. The OAN plans to accomplish this by helping members audit their energy use and by developing an open system of communication where nurseries can learn from each other and find incentives for making changes. Currently, eight nurseries are actively participating in the program, but the OAN wants to expand that to thirty. Active participation means that companies agree to make progress on the "25 percent in ten years" goal; to share energy audit data with the OAN and its partners; and to allow the overall project results to be made public through videos, presentations, and published case studies. In return the nurseries get a free energy audit, technical assistance in planning and implementing projects, and help in identifying and applying for grants and other financial assistance to offset project costs. The hope, says Rideout, is that in two years the OAN "can better understand energy measurement on-farm and begin publishing findings."

The OAN has published a sustainability road map, which considers the future (to 2020) of the Oregon nursery industry relative to the environmental concerns of energy, climate, water, and waste. Published in May 2011 (and available online), the guide sets industry goals, documents the needed resources and partnerships, and describes the likely impacts of better environmental stewardship. The OAN is also partnering with other organizations to help nurseries certify through the third-party organization Food Alliance and the nonprofit Salmon-Safe, which focuses on local water quality (see chapter 7). And the OAN is currently seeking funding for a true life-cycle assessment of the nursery industry: what it really takes—how much water, fuel, emissions—to grow and install plants. That would be powerful data.

Asked what designers and owners can do to promote sustainability in the green industry, Rideout has a simple answer: they should support nurseries that are taking steps to improve their environmental pedigree. That means asking a few questions, and maybe touring facilities (see "Questions for growers" in chapter 8).

Ultimately, the OAN's research, which is unequaled by any other nursery industry organization, is finding that growers can actually save money through environmental initiatives. Saving fuel and water, it seems, not only helps the environment but also the bottom line.

5: Water and Fertilizer: Water, Water Everywhere

In the late 2000s, the orange juice giant Tropicana, in an effort to improve its green performance, analyzed the environmental impact of all of its practices. What it found was that the top negative environmental activity, by some margin, was the application of synthetic fertilizer on its fields. That is due primarily to the fact that it takes a lot of high-carbon natural gas to make the common ammonia-based fertilizers the agriculture industry uses, and that fertilizer releases nitrous oxide, a greenhouse gas, into the environment. As a result of that analysis, PepsiCo, Tropicana's parent company, is experimenting with lower-carbon fertilizers, including one option that includes some organic products.[1]

Howard Garrett points to the Tropicana study as proof that change is needed—not just in orange groves but in landscape management in general. Garrett is a Dallas-based arborist and horticulturist, and he is more commonly known as the Dirt Doctor. He has written fourteen books on organic gardening and nursery practices, consults with landscape architects and corporations on organic maintenance, and has a radio show syndicated in 150 markets. He says that the main problem with synthetic fertilizers is that they don't effectively fertilize a plant.[2] Plants need various minerals and organic materials and even micro-organisms present naturally in soil. Synthetic fertilizer, which is essentially a soluble salt, does damage to the soil biology, thereby necessitating more fertilizer application. This is true both in a nursery and in a completed landscape. It also provides very little actual nutrient benefit for the plant, since it can volatize into the air and is deliberately designed to be water soluble (for absorption by plants), so it can run off with the next watering. And because synthetic fertilizer is a petroleum product, it comes with all the fossil fuel concerns listed in chapter 3.

The effect of fertilizer on the environment is most typically seen in waterways. Fertilizers contain mostly phosphorous materials (so-called triple-super phosphate is the latest breakthrough) and nitrogen, both of which cause algae blooms in lakes and streams. Phosphate also wants to combine with just about everything in the environment, so it sequesters minerals, making them unavailable to plants and aquatic animals.

Nurseries, in particular, use a lot of fertilizer—too much, according to Christa Orum-Keller of Midwest Groundcovers, and too much water. Most nursery and growing-yard irrigation consists of high-mounted spray heads, which quite literally throw water to the wind. Water not lost to immediate evaporation might hit plants, but it also might hit the ground and run off to the nearest stream. This is especially wasteful in arid environments, where water is hard won from depleting aquifers or distant shrinking reservoirs. In cases where irrigation water is spiked with fertilizer, a not uncommon practice, all that runoff is then laden with chemicals.

Once a landscape project is installed, fertilization continues, along with, often, chemical pest and weed control. On-site irrigation, too, throws more water to the wind.

Organic fertilizers

The opposite of synthetic fertilizer is an organic fertilizer. Garrett defines organic fertilizers as any product that will help the health of the plant while also benefiting the soil itself. Perhaps the best option is a liquid application called compost tea. Lambert Landscape Company makes its own compost tea with rainwater it collects from its building roofs (see the case study in this chapter). The tea is the company's standard maintenance technique, and it has been since the 1980s when Lambert went completely organic. Compost tea is a mixture of cow, bird, and plant compost (some of Lambert's plant compost comes from the company's own green waste) mixed with some kind of sugar (molasses, fish, kelp, or unsellable fruit).

The recipe for Howard Garrett's "Garrett Juice" is available online and is another option for organic fertilizing.[3] It includes compost tea blended with apple cider vinegar, molasses, fish meal, and seaweed. Garret also recommends adding ground-up rock, ideally green sand or lava sand, to the soil as a top dressing.

Though organic fertilization is used only rarely, MESA Design Group has worked with Garrett to modify its standard specifications to require organic practices in installation and maintenance (see the case study in chapter 8).

Organic fertilization has many benefits. Foremost is that healthy soil means healthy plants. Compost tea doesn't merely fertilize plants, because it also puts beneficial bacteria into the soil, which will perpetuate themselves and create nutrients for the plants on an ongoing basis. That means owners don't have to fertilize as often. Also, because plants aren't struggling with salt in the soil, they are less thirsty. Garrett estimates organic fertilizers can cut water use by as much as 50 percent, which equates directly to cost savings for the owner.

Catchment, reuse, and efficient distribution

The conventional water cycle in a nursery goes like this: well water or municipal water is sprayed on growing fields by overhead sprayers, the water not used by plants runs off (usually now impregnated with fertilizer), and new water is brought in to water the next time. That is quite literally like flushing money down the toilet. Water and fertilizer are significant expenses for any nursery or growing yard, and those costs are likely to increase as water becomes more scarce and oil prices rise. The water cycle could be better managed with a closed system, like the one at Midwest Groundcovers (see the case study in this chapter).

At the front end of the cycle, water doesn't have to come from the ground or from municipal pipes. Christy Webber Landscapes (CWL) has a cistern that catches rainwater from its maintenance building roof for use in watering plants on-site and for washing vehicles. One Green World (OGW) has installed a European-made steel storage tank with a capacity of an acre-foot of water, which it plans to use for irrigation. Lambert catches water from its shop roof in a 30,000-gallon cistern and uses that water to make compost tea. Despite making 1,600 gallons of tea every day for application on the nearly 300 acres of landscape Lambert maintains, and despite being in relatively dry north Texas, the cistern has never run dry.

The next key step is to rely more on drip irrigation than on spray heads. Drip irrigation delivers water directly to plant roots rather than to leaves and the air. This can be a more expensive proposition to install, but nurseries will save money on water in the long run. Several of the green industry companies profiled in this book use drip irrigation extensively.

Irrigation systems

Most landscapes, once they are installed, are regularly watered with in-ground irrigation systems. The most environmentally sound option is to plant species tolerant of local water conditions and eliminate irrigation entirely, but that is not always possible. Luckily, significant advances have come over the past decade in irrigation technology. Irrigation companies seem invested in improving efficiency, likely since they know that they can save their clients money. Irrigation is itself a topic well covered in books and articles, but suffice it to say here that spending a little extra on a top-of-the-line irrigation system will pay dividends in water use and cost savings almost immediately.

Most irrigation companies make some kind of ET system—the ET stands for evapotranspiration. Such systems go beyond simply sensing whether it is currently raining or not. Instead they use data gathered on-site or through remote weather stations to more accurately measure local weather conditions, actual soil moisture, or the rate of water loss from plants and the earth. Though more expensive up front, these systems save water and money.

Checklist

Plants are a critical aspect of most landscape projects, and plants need water and nutrients—as they grow from seeds to saleable size, when they are installed, and for their entire lives. Landscape architects, owners, and even installers often have little control over how a plant is grown for sale; and designers, installers, and growers do not generally control how a plant is maintained after the punch list. All creators and stewards of landscapes can, however, take more control, through specifications, changing internal practices, and the selection and recommendation of growers and maintainers.

The discussion here enters into the well-debated and well-documented discussion of plant maintenance. Few landscape architects and even owners wade into this area, instead leaving it to those who maintain plants as their sole business, to university extension services that study growing and maintenance methods of everything from grass to apple trees, and to a few specialist designers who have made plant maintenance a key part of their businesses and are sought after as consultants nationwide. This book won't delve deeply into the question of maintenance, but there are still things owners and designers can do and consider when it comes to projects large and small.

Also keep in mind that water management systems like rain gardens, permeable paving, and green roofs are types of landscapes that manage the water a site generates (through runoff or rainfall). Xeriscaping, or the selection of drought-resistant plants, fall into this same category. None of these are addressed here because the following checklist deals with how green industry professionals, owners, and landscape architects can help reduce water use in the growing and maintenance of plants—any plants, even green-roof or drought-tolerant plants, which still require water and nutrients to grow and survive. As described in chapter 1, this book is concerned with reducing the water and fertilizer impacts of any type of landscape.

Creating plans and specifications

❏ **Consider specifying organic maintenance and installation.** Lambert in Texas achieves exceptional results with a wholly organic maintenance regime. But Pacific in Oregon, one of the greenest management companies around, has decided that a blend of organic and synthetic fertilizer works best. MESA Design Group has written a specification that includes organic installation and maintenance practices but admits not every client is willing to step away from conventional practices. Landscape architects and owners interested in an organic maintenance regime will have to work together to establish a level of comfort and expectation for the project.

❏ **Extend the required maintenance period.** Specifying organic soil preparation and initial maintenance could be done on almost any project. Ongoing maintenance, however, is more difficult to control for the landscape architect. If designers and their clients desire organic maintenance,

it will be beneficial to extend the required maintenance period included in the project bid from one year to three or more years. This will ensure the contractor spends time and effort getting the soil prepared and plants installed properly, because that will make plant success easier down the line. True, this will increase "construction" costs, but that will be made up by the elimination of maintenance costs for those years included in the bid. This is often done for restoration projects, especially in the upper Midwest. As with other unconventional practices, contractors should be alerted to this aspect of a bid, so they don't get stuck with extra costs later for work they did not understand was included.

❏ **Specify the most advanced irrigation system available.** Irrigation may not always be permanently necessary, but when it is, advanced systems can significantly reduce water use and save an owner money in the long run. Pacific has had success with weather-based systems. A green roof in Minneapolis features sensors that mimic plant leaves, to get a better picture of actual moisture loss from the plants themselves.[4] Such systems allow irrigation to be used only when truly necessary, which saves (often potable) water. Inherent in this checklist item is the need for landscape architects and owners to take a more active role in the design and specification of irrigation, something often left to the irrigation companies themselves or to an irrigation contractor.

❑ **Specify certified plant material.** Where available, Salmon-Safe, USDA Organic, or Veriflora certifications provide some environmental insurance. At the very least, any certification program will require a company to document a variety of inputs and outputs—data not otherwise typically available. Though none of these certification systems is perfect, it would be easy to hold a contractor to them through project submittals, should an owner or designer choose to use one. You can read more on certifications in chapter 7.

Working with green industry professionals

❑ **Choose growers with efficient water and fertilizer systems.** When landscape architects and owners have the luxury of choosing where their plants are grown, they should consider the watering and fertilizing practices of their growers. Catchment and reuse of irrigation water is entirely possible. Though catchment is required by many local laws, reuse is less commonly practiced, meaning nurseries continually draw fresh well water. Without reuse, any fertilizer added to irrigation water is lost, possibly even sent downstream into the environment. In addition, most watering is done with high-mounted spray heads, which is a less efficient distribution system—as far as the amount of water actually delivered to plant roots—than drip irrigation. Owners and landscape architects should consider a grower's water and fertilizer systems as part of the total picture of the grower's environmental credibility (see "Questions for growers" in chapter 8).

❑ **Choose management companies willing to consider organic maintenance.** Landscape maintainers may be reluctant to provide warranties on plant material if they are required to practice organic maintenance. Unless the directive for organic maintenance comes from the owner or the manager itself, there may be significant pushback. However, by using long-term relationships with trusted installers and maintainers, landscape architects can also work with those companies to experiment with organic maintenance, likely working together with owners to absolve management companies from some warranty requirements. This has to be a three-way partnership—landscape architect, management company, and owner—and may be an ongoing experiment. However, this is an excellent opportunity for designers and owners to learn about organics and about landscape maintenance in general, and the manager may learn inexpensive techniques they will apply to other sites.

Changing internal practices

❑ **Use drip irrigation as much as possible.** Drip irrigation puts water nearer to a plant's roots and reduces wasted overspray. As a more efficient water distribution system it also has fertilizer benefits, whenever nutrients are delivered to plants in irrigation water. Various types of drip irrigation can deliver water to field-grown plants and plants in pots. It can be used where needed, relocated, and, at the end of its useful life, recycled.

❑ **Consider organic maintenance.** Growers, installers, and managers often have tried-and-true methods for making their plants thrive, but experimentation is worth the effort. There are organic gardening resources for nearly every region and plant type, and the components of organic fertilizer are widely available. Having either organically grown plants or the option for an organic maintenance regime may also be a powerful marketing opportunity.

❑ **Pursue certification, or purchase certified plants.** Several certification programs apply directly to nurseries. Though Veriflora and USDA Organic certifications may be more effort than they are worth, all nurseries and growers in the Pacific Northwest should pursue Salmon-Safe certification as proof they are stewarding the local watershed. Similarly, owners, landscape installers, and management companies should consider purchasing Veriflora-certified plants whenever possible. These are beginning to become available at larger garden centers and do ensure at least some environmental improvement over conventionally grown plants. Read more about certifications in chapter 7.

❑ **Install the most efficient irrigation system available.** Owners, landscape architects, and landscape installers and managers often work together to select, program, and operate an irrigation system. Any new irrigation system should utilize some type of local or regional data—whether gained from weather stations or from the site itself—to automatically adjust watering regimens. Though likely more expensive than a more conventional programmable system with a rain sensor, a data-driven system will save water and money in the near and long terms.

CASE STUDY: MIDWEST GROUNDCOVERS

Midwest Groundcovers (MG) produces about 12 million plants each year on 120 acres west of Chicago. It grows shrubs and perennials, including forty varieties of sedum aimed at the green-roof market, native plants for the "American Beauties" program of the National Wildlife Federation, and planting modules for green-roof installations. The company is the labor of love of Peter Orum, a native Dane who has brought some Scandinavian sustainability to the Midwest. Orum started the company in the early 1980s and it now employs around two hundred seasonal employees and fifty year-round staff.

MG previously occupied a site in the Chicago suburb of St. Charles, Illinois. The company was outgrowing that space, and a fortuitous buyout of part of its property for a highway project facilitated a move to the current site in more rural Virgil. The company has employed sustainable practices since its inception, like reusing plastic containers, but the new site offered the chance to rethink the entire way the business is organized.

The landscape architect Chris Lannert, who founded the Lannert Group, has known Orum for thirty years; they met

Midwest Groundcovers' facility is divided into three separate nursery areas, reducing vehicle miles. (Midwest Groundcovers)

on a small landscaping job early in Lannert's career. In 2001, Orum hired Lannert to master plan their new container nursery and corporate headquarters. The landscape architect immediately recognized the potential to make the company's production more efficient. "This is really an industrial process," describes Lannert, "but they don't make widgets, they make plants. When you machine a part and you have scrap metal, you don't just throw it away, you gather it up, you melt it back down, and you pour a new part. They could do the same thing with all of their nutrients, with all of their water."

That comprehensive reuse would be difficult across 120 acres, so the site is broken down into four growing areas, each ranging from between 25 to 30 acres. This is the genius of the design: each growing area (three are built) is self-contained. Each has its own shop, vehicles, water retention ponds, filtration and nutrification system, and employees. This cuts on-site vehicle miles roughly in half.

The planning and design process took five years, including a year of negotiation with Kane County to get a variance to place what is considered an industrial business in an agricultural area. That negotiation was helped by the fact that MG would install vegetated windbreaks, which also shield the site from view. The windbreaks cost money, but they help reduce water use by blocking desiccating winds and they protect seasonal greenhouses from damage.

Another major showpiece is the drainage, irrigation, and fertilization system. Yes, that's one system—the three are inextricably linked at MG, something not often the case at nurseries. MG fertilizes primarily through its irrigation water, something it has done for twenty-five years. "Every drop of water that falls on the developed part of the property," explained Christa Orum-Keller, MG's vice president (who is

Midwest Groundcovers uses drip irrigation in many of its growing fields.

also a registered landscape architect), "moves to detention basins and is used for irrigation." This is also true of the irrigation water itself. Essentially, each growing lot is made of free-draining aggregate, like that found under permeable pavement. Water moves downward into the aggregate and enters a perforated pipe, through which it makes its way to swales, then to large storage ponds.

All of Midwest Groundcovers' greenhouses have underdrains that bring unused irrigation water back to holding ponds for reuse.

Midwest Groundcovers draws rainwater and unused irrigation water from holding ponds, analyzes nutrient content, and pumps it back into the irrigation system. (Midwest Groundcovers)

Near each system of ponds (one for each growing area) is a highly complex pumping system. Water is drawn from the ponds and is tested for its nutrient content. Fertilizer is only added if necessary. Then the water is provided to the plants through aerial sprays or, sometimes, more expensive (but more efficient) drip irrigation. The whole site is graded, according to Lannert, to move water from the growing areas into the ponds then back to the growing areas in the form of irrigation.

According to Orum-Keller both water and fertilizer are resources that can be reclaimed, thereby saving money. She says

Though Midwest Groundcovers uses overhead sprays in some of its growing yards, any extra water flows back to holding ponds for reuse. (Midwest Groundcovers)

reclaiming both water and fertilizer, Orum-Keller estimates that the company cuts its fertilizer use and cost in half.

In the center of the complex is a facility operated by a separate company, Midwest Trading (though MG and Midwest Trading share a board and owners). This company makes soil and mulch for conventional landscape applications and green roofs. MG piles all its green waste in a single location, and when the pile reaches a certain height, MG works with Midwest Trading to reuse it in some way. How the waste is used depends on the waste itself. Woody materials might get chipped and turned into mulch. Diseased material can be ground up and put on a fallow field as an organic amendment—as long as no plants will grow there in the near future. Whatever happens to the green waste, all of it is reused somehow within the nursery operation.

In addition to its compact growing areas, drainage and irrigation system, and green-waste recycling, MG allows customers to return plastic plant pots from any grower, which they bale on site, reducing the cost to have them recycled. It reuses some of these pots as is—simply knocking out the dirt and replanting. At its growing field in Michigan, all the plastic pots go to East Jordan Plastics, a pioneering company that is making new plant pots out of recycled plant pots (MG's Michigan site also buys recycled pots from East Jordan, closing the loop

that's not common practice: "I think a lot of small growers are just throwing fertilizer on the plants and not putting much science into it." She feels MG's system makes sense from both a cost and an environmental perspective. "Fertilizer is expensive," she stresses, "so if you're just throwing it out there because you think it might help, you're throwing money away. It's not a good thing to have more fertilizer in the water than you need." By on its own plastic). MG reuses its white plastic greenhouse covers three times and then recycles them. And the company's "energy committee" is considering wind and solar power generation, electric site vehicles, and a new geothermal greenhouse for the fourth growing area. "At our old site," explains Orum-Keller, "[the elements of sustainability] were a little bit here and a little bit there." The new campus brings all of MG's environmental practices together in an integrated system.

Lambert Landscape Company captures rainwater in a large cistern and uses it to make compost tea. (Lambert Landscape Company)

CASE STUDY:
LAMBERT LANDSCAPE COMPANY

Lambert Landscape Company designs, builds, and maintains high-end residential landscapes in primarily Classical styles. Projects feature custom-designed urns carved in Italy, carefully clipped boxwood geometries, hand-laid mosaics, and other craft-driven elements. Though these designs set the company apart, Lambert's maintenance practices are equally groundbreaking. The company's staff rake by hand and trim hedges with hand-held clippers instead of motorized ones (the company believes gas-powered clippers injure plants). And Lambert's maintenance practices are also completely organic, relying principally on compost tea made on-site with water captured from building roofs.

Lambert started up in Shreveport, Louisiana, in the early 1900s and opened its Dallas location in the 1930s. Over the years, the company has collaborated on residential projects with big-name landscape architects like Thomas Church, employed the eventual founders of the major design firm JJR, and brought to Dallas the azaleas that trace the city's creeks with color in the spring. Today, Lambert has about 175 employees, designs dozens of new gardens each year, and maintains nearly 200 private residences.

The company (and its subsidiaries Moore Tree Care, Moore Life, Moore Lawn and Garden, and Moore Commercial Landscape Management) went organic in the late 1980s. This required not just a change in what it was using to fertilize plants and control pests, but it needed a whole new way of thinking. "Organic does not work reactively," says Judy Joseph, Lambert's director of garden services, who coordinates the company's twenty-one maintenance crews. For pest and disease control, Lambert uses a variety of weapons, including compost, Bt bacteria (*Bacillus thuringiensis*, a common soil-dwelling organism regularly used as a pesticide), orange oil, wasps, and ladybugs. For fertilization, landscapes get dousings of compost tea about seven times per year (the tea, essentially the consistency of water, is sprayed on with a garden hose attached to a tank truck). A horticultural calendar, developed in-house, helps crews anticipate threats through comparisons between this year, last year, and a ten-year average. The calendar lets the company get ahead of likely outbreaks of nasties like webworms and chinch bugs.

Lambert staff admit that organic practices don't always work as fast as chemicals would. Organic fertilization is designed to enrich soil biology rather than boost growth

Lambert makes compost tea daily and applies it to landscapes as an organic fertilizer.

immediately; organic pest control is meant to interrupt the spread of bugs by disrupting their life cycle, rather than by eradicating them outright. However, the company feels organic practices work at two scales of environmental benefit. Firstly, the plant itself will be healthier in the long run and will require less water and, overall, less fertilizer than one

The tea is applied by hoses from tanker trucks.

ing Dallas's infrequent but torrential storms. The water makes up most of the compost tea, which Lambert brews just about every day. Steve Gaharan is director of Moore Tree Care and Moore Life (the maintenance side of Lambert), and he oversees the compost tea system, which is essentially a collection of vats and vessels all connected together by black tubing. A few pumps sit on the ground, out in the open.

The key to the tea is the compost mix. It took plenty of experimentation to get just the right blend that Gaharan feels has the optimum nutrient profile. The base of the mix includes composted cow manure, bird droppings, and plant waste. Then Lambert adds a sugar source, either molasses, or something called "harvest to harvest": ugly or oversized fruit not fit for sale, which is pureed and mixed with fish or kelp. Essentially, the composted products bring beneficial organisms to the table, and the sugars feed them, so they multiply prodigiously.

The compost is placed in a hopper, mixed with collected rainwater to make a slurry, and aerated. Pumps pull the slurry up into the tea machine, a 1,600-gallon plastic vat with a cone-shaped bottom. At the top of the vat the slurry passes through a hydro-cyclone, which slings the organisms off the solid compost and deposits them in the water that is slowly collecting below. The large particles settle to the bottom of the vat, while

fed with synthetics. Second, the entire earth benefits from reduced fossil fuel use and environmental pollutants entering the environment.

The cornerstone of Lambert's organic program is a 30,000-gallon steel cistern, which sits in the equipment-staging parking lot just to the side of a long shed-roof building. This cistern captures rainwater that falls on the shop roof durthe remaining water, now impregnated with millions of beneficial bacteria, is drawn off into tanker trucks through hoses connected to the side of the vat.

Gaharan occasionally takes samples to a microscope—that's also how he created the best mix—to verify the quality of the tea: the more critters, the better the blend.

Lambert buys the harvest-to-harvest, the molasses, and the cow and poultry compost, but the company has a hand in making the plant compost. Years ago, the company's crews would return to headquarters with plastic bags of grass clippings and prunings from trees and shrubs and pile them at the back of the yard. A conventional garbage hauler would take that green waste to a landfill. Today, the company separates its green waste in the field. Crews bring the woody cuttings back for chipping and pack the grass in burlap sacks. Another company picks up the chips and the grass (bags and all—burlap is compostable) and hauls them to a compost yard. The same company sells back to Lambert the plant compost used in the compost tea, as well as a composted soil blend called pH Revitalizer that Lambert uses on most projects. The green waste—some of it at least—ends up in a closed-loop system, with Lambert's cuttings being composted, turned into tea, and applied onto plants, which are then cut again. Gaharan laments a little that he has to pay both for the green waste pickup and for the resultant soil, but he feels this is a better arrangement at the moment than composting the waste on-site, which takes plenty of space and effort.

At the core of Lambert's philosophy is an understanding of the soil. The tea the company applies is meant to improve soil, thereby improving plant health. This is a different perspective than focusing on the plant first. Lambert staff told me that the standard green industry practice, both in growing yards and in maintained landscapes, is to "blast plants with fertilizer and water." The company feels this creates a situation where plants will always be dependent on that blasting and will decline once maintenance slacks off. It also wastes resources. Once the soil is healthy, says Lambert, plants can truly thrive.

6: Green Waste: Throwing Away the Golden Goose

Every trade in the green industry generates landscape waste. Nurseries wind up with piles of old plants, trimmings, and pots of soil. Landscape contractors haul away remnants of an existing landscape: sod, shrubs, old mulch, and even trees. Landscape management companies generate tree and shrub prunings, grass clippings, and old plants to be replaced with new ones. This is collectively known as green waste. Where does it go? That depends on location. In Minnesota, Pennsylvania, South Carolina, New Hampshire and other states (see the list on page 72), most of that green waste must, by law, not enter a landfill or incinerator (the laws vary from state to state, but in general the states on the list forbid landfilling of most organic yard and construction waste). Elsewhere, it is probably plowed under with the kitchen scraps, construction debris, and broken toys.[1]

The latter situation is a problem because green waste is easily compostable. It can become new, nutrient-rich soil. It can form a part of the never-ending cycle of organic material: soil begets plants, which die and beget more soil. Again, there are no figures for the amount of green waste generated nationwide, but consider a single site, the AmberGlen campus managed by Pacific Landscape Management (see the case study in chapter 3). Through lawn mowing, native landscape cutting, plant replacement, and general pruning, that 217-acre site generates 15,000 cubic yards of green waste per year.[2] That's about the equivalent of a football field stacked twelve feet deep with landscaping refuse.

The main problem for landscape companies, namely installers, is that the green waste needs to be separated from all the inorganic stuff like plant pots and busted-out concrete. That adds work, and in places where the landfilling of green waste is allowed, nothing is typically done to separate these types of waste. Sadly, Florida recently rolled back its law requiring composting (despite even a gubernatorial veto), primarily on the promise by the waste management industry that more methane-generated electricity could be produced at landfills if more green waste were deposited there.[3]

Compost, compost, compost

There is really just one environmentally appropriate solution for green waste: compost it. Some nurseries, installers, and managers are beginning to compost their own waste or to make arrangements with composting companies (see the case studies on One Green World, Lambert, and Midwest Groundcovers).

By far the most efficient method of composting, though, especially for smaller installers, maintenance companies, and some owners, is to bring green waste to a private facility. True, the drop-off costs money, but so does separating and dropping materials at a landfill. The process of making compost seems simple—pile up the waste, make sure there's enough water and air circulation, and wait—but managing a good compost heap can become a full-time job. There are also some economies of scale, namely the fact that the heap must reach a temperature of about 130 degrees for seven days in order to kill pathogens: a tricky proposition for a small heap with limited oversight.

The compost can, of course, be used in a variety of ways: as a component of planting soil, for compost tea, or even as erosion control in compost socks.

CHECKLIST

This checklist boils down to one major goal: making sure green waste is composted rather than landfilled. Owners, green industry professionals, and landscape architects can do this in a variety of ways outlined in this checklist. However, because some states and municipalities have existing laws preventing lawn and landscape waste from being deposited in landfills, this checklist is primarily for those in other areas.

Creating plans and specifications

❏ **Require green-waste composting.** As discussed in the checklist on plastic pots, landscape architects and owners can require submittals for a variety of construction practices, including waste disposal. Composting facilities, like landfills, often charge for green waste drop-off, and a landscape contractor could simply submit the drop-off receipt. As with plastic pots, the specification could include penalties, just as it would for other errors in performance, disposal, or paperwork. If installers are composting their own waste, the landscape architect or owner may need to make a site visit to verify the existence of composting facilities.

Working with green industry professionals

❑ **Ask for disposal documentation.** After a project is installed, responsibility generally falls to the owner to ensure that a maintenance company continues to drop off green waste at a composting facility rather than at a landfill. This can be monitored by requiring monthly documentation along with invoicing.

❑ **Choose and recommend growers and installers with environmental credibility.** Some growers and contractors, even in areas where composting is not required, are keeping their green waste out of landfills, either by composting and reusing it themselves or by dropping it at a private composting facility. The treatment of green waste is one of the many things an owner or landscape architect should ask about when determining whether to recommend a company based on its overall environmental performance (see "Questions for growers" and "Questions for installers" in chapter 8).

Changing internal practices

❑ **Compost green waste.** Obviously, composting is what this chapter is driving at, and there are many ways green industry professionals and owners who maintain their own sites can accomplish this. The easiest way is to bring green waste to a commercial composting facility. These facilities are carefully managed to ensure the compost is free of pathogens and has the correct texture and degree of composition. Nurseries, owners, and landscape companies might also consider maintaining their own compost piles. This will eliminate drop-off fees and can generate free mulch or soil additives. However, a compost pile requires management, which will necessitate staff time and resources. Organizations that regularly generate waste, like a landscape management company or an owner maintaining its own site, could also consider a partnership with a waste collection company, like the one Lambert established. Whatever the arrangement, in no case should green waste be sent to a landfill—it should instead become new soil through composting.

Advocacy

❑ **Push for and support composting laws.** In places where compost can be legally landfilled, landscape architects should work through their professional organization and, ideally, with the local green industry organization to pass legislation banning that practice. Required composting is the norm in twenty-four states. This has little effect on the green industry (namely because everyone has to do it, so everyone bears the same cost of disposal) and supports a partner industry: the businesses that compost green waste and food waste and turn it into new soil. In the long run, landscape architects won't have to convince every client, and owners won't have to hound every contractor to compost if they were required to do so by law.

LIST OF STATES WITH COMPOSTING LAWS, AS OF MARCH 2011[4]

Arkansas	New Hampshire
Connecticut	New Jersey
Delaware	North Carolina
Illinois	North Dakota
Indiana	Ohio
Iowa	Pennsylvania
Maryland	Rhode Island
Massachusetts	South Carolina
Michigan	South Dakota
Minnesota	Vermont
Missouri	West Virginia
Nebraska	Wisconsin

7: Rating Systems and the Green Industry

It seems like everything has a rating these days: movies can be PG-13, fresh produce can be organic, eggs can be Grade A, appliances can be EnergyStar, chickens can be free range, and buildings can be LEED Gold. The last rating in that list, the U.S. Green Building Council (USGBC)'s Leadership in Energy and Environmental Design (LEED®),[1] has become the primary way buildings and their associated landscapes are rated for their environmental performance. There are plenty of other green building guidelines, but LEED has become the standard of late. Though primarily a tool for building managers and architects, LEED has collected hundreds of landscape architects to its side, as well, and does include a wide array of site-related requirements.

A different site-specific rating system called the Sustainable Sites Initiative (SITES™) is currently in the works. An interdisciplinary effort by the American Society of Landscape Architects, the Lady Bird Johnson Wildflower Center in Austin, Texas, and the United States Botanic Garden, this system will establish voluntary environmental performance guidelines for projects without buildings or where site dominates—projects that are primarily the bailiwick of landscape architects.

On the nursery side, several smaller programs, some regional in scope, are looking at plant materials and growing practices with an eye toward social and environmental stewardship.

Landscape architects, owners, and green industry professionals can use these various rating systems to improve the environmental performance of how their projects are grown and installed. This chapter looks at seven different systems (beginning with LEED). Each section gives a brief overview of the purpose of the rating system, then considers how it might apply to the subject of environmental performance of landscape creation, installation, and maintenance.

LEED®

This ubiquitous rating system debuted in 2000, and its now-famous point system classifies buildings as Certified, Silver, Gold, or Platinum based on their overall environmental performance. LEED features nine different systems, depending on the type of building: Homes, Commercial Interiors, Core & Shell, New Construction, Schools, Retail: New Construction, Retail: Commercial Interiors, Existing Buildings: Operations and Maintenance, and Neighborhood Development. To become certified, a building must document its environmental performance on a variety of items, winning points for meeting requirements. Achieving certain point totals entitles a building to advertise itself as LEED and put up the familiar three-leaf logo.

Using LEED to encourage environmental landscape practices

The LEED rating system only applies to projects seeking LEED certification. Typically, such projects will involve interdisciplinary work in which the landscape will be only a portion. A landscape architect will be responsible for suggesting ways to achieve points with landscape design, installation, and maintenance, and for documenting how those points are, in fact, achieved. Most of the different LEED ratings systems provide points for landscape interventions within the broad Sustainable Sites category. Included here are such actions as preserving existing habitat, managing storm water, and reducing the heat island effect. As discussed in chapter 1, while these are all important goals of environmentally sound landscape architecture, they have little to do with installation and maintenance and more to do with design (rain-garden plants can still be grown, installed, and maintained in an environmentally unfriendly way even though a rain garden itself will provides environmental benefits).

The LEED for Homes system takes a more comprehensive look at landscaping, and it is covered in the next section. In the other LEED rating systems, the only credit item specifically dealing with growing, installing, and maintaining landscapes is "Water Efficient Landscaping" (which appears in most of the different certification systems). This credit provides two points for the reduction of potable water for irrigation by 50 percent through any of a variety of means, including irrigation efficiency (four points are given for the total elimination of potable water use). Specifying a highly efficient, weather-based irrigation system would meet the intent of this credit.

The other opportunity for gaining LEED points through environmentally sound green industry practices is in the "Innovation in Design" credit category. This is a catch-all credit designed to encourage new ideas that may not be otherwise specifically addressed in the rating system. The requirements of the credit state that the innovation must "achieve significant, measurable environmental performance." (This statement appears more or less verbatim in each of the many LEED rating systems.) Landscape architects, working with green industry companies, may find documentable innovations, such as organic plant growing, plant pot and green waste management, fuel efficiency in installation, or perhaps an integrated "environmental landscape installation" innovation. Though innovation points are awarded at the discretion of USGBC reviewers, they could be especially achievable if these are practices that landscape architects are already encouraging.

In short, USGBC does not award significant points for environmental landscape installation and maintenance (most credits deal with the design of the landscape—not a topic covered in this book). However, at the beginning of LEED projects while the design team is brainstorming about potential credits, landscape architects should raise the possibility of these points, because efficient irrigation can actually save a client money over time and environmental installation practices may not cost much more than conventional methods. These could be several easily achievable points that don't significantly increase the cost of a project.

Using LEED for Homes to encourage environmental landscape practices

Like the other LEED rating systems, LEED for Homes addresses landscape installation and maintenance practices primarily through irrigation-efficiency requirements. However, this system provides more specific detail on water efficiency, and it also requires homeowner or site manager education and training on irrigation and other building and landscape systems. In addition to the credits described in detail below, LEED for Homes also provides innovation credits, like those described above.

- **Credit WE (Water Efficiency) 1.1: Rainwater Harvesting System.** LEED for Homes offers up to four points for installing a catchment system for rainwater that allows that captured water to be used for irrigation and indoor water use.

- **Credit WE 2.1: High-Efficiency Irrigation System.** Up to three points are available for installing an irrigation system with a variety of listed features. Though ET and weather-based systems are mentioned, it is entirely possible to achieve all three LEED points with a somewhat conventional system that includes, say, a central shut-off valve (one point), a timer controller (a second point), and check valves in the spray heads (a third point). This credit also offers points for drip irrigation, separate zonation for different planting types, and high-efficiency spray nozzles.

- **Credit WE 2.2: Third-Party Inspection.** In addition to the three points available for the system itself, another point is given for the postinstallation inspection of the irrigation system.

- **Credit AE (Awareness and Education) 1: Education of the Homeowner or Tenant.** LEED for Homes offers up to two points for educating the incoming resident and the community at large about a home's green features. Though the focus here is obviously on the building itself, certain landscape maintenance practices—namely the irrigation system—must be incorporated into a project maintenance manual and on-site, in-person training. Another option in this credit is to perform some type of public outreach, like a public open house, an informational website, or a newspaper article.

- **Credit AE 2: Education of Building Manager.** This credit operates exactly like AE 1, but instead the person who will operate the building and landscape is educated, in cases where that person will not live in the home. The public awareness campaign is not an option under this credit.

LEED® Canada

LEED Canada is managed by the Canada Green Building Council and is based on USGBC's LEED rating system.[2] Though there are some technical differences between the two systems—to address differences in Canadian codes and climate—the vast majority of the prerequisites and credits are almost identical.

The various items in the LEED for Homes system also hold true for the Canadian program. In the other rating systems, the two LEED credits that offer points for landscape installation and management are also present in the LEED Canada system: water-efficient landscaping, and innovation in design. Both are applied the same way (two points for a 50 percent irrigation potable water use reduction, four points for a 100 percent reduction, and discretionary points for innovative items).

Sustainable Sites Initiative (SITES™)

This site-based rating system officially kicked off in 2005 and is currently evaluating a set of pilot projects nationwide, in hopes of releasing a final rating system in 2013. USGBC, according to the SITES website, anticipates incorporating SITES into its family of rating systems.[3] Like LEED, SITES is built around a series of credits, for which points are awarded, leading to eventual certification. In early 2012, SITES announced its first certified projects. These projects were evaluated according to pilot guidelines completed in 2009. The SITES team is currently working toward revising the 2009 guidelines and issuing new ones in 2013. Though it is likely many of the new prerequisites and credits will be created in a similar spirit to the 2009 version, the discussion of specific SITES items below does not include prerequisite and credit numbers, which may change.

Using SITES to encourage environmental landscape practices

SITES has specific prerequisites and available credits related to how a site is constructed and maintained. The following credits directly apply:

- **Prerequisite: Reduce potable water use for landscape irrigation by 50 percent from established baselines.** Because this is a prerequisite, any project seeking SITES certification will need to accomplish that reduction. SITES allows the reduction to be made (similarly to LEED) through any of eight factors, including irrigation efficiency. The SITES guidebook specifically references drip irrigation and climate-based controllers.

- **Credit: Reduce potable water use for landscape irrigation by 75 percent or more from the established baseline.** Building on the above prerequisite, points are available for projects that reduce irrigation water use even further, either through (again) irrigation efficiency or the use of gray water, captured rainwater, or air conditioner condensate. Specification and installation of a truly innovative system could garner up to five points.

- **Credit: Protect and enhance on-site water resources and receiving water quality.** Though this credit primarily deals with treatment of runoff, it does make specific reference to maintenance practices, including reducing fertilizers and pesticides and avoiding maintenance and fueling of construction equipment on-site. Improving construction and maintenance practices as described in this book could assist in gaining points for this credit.

- **Credit: Support sustainable practices in plant produc-**

tion. This credit provides three points if 90 percent of purchased plants come from businesses that employ at least six of eight stated principles. Those principles are summarized as follows:

> Use of sustainable soil amendments
>
> Reduction of irrigation runoff
>
> Generation or purchase of renewable energy
>
> Reduction in overall energy use
>
> Use of integrated pest management (which, though SITES does not specifically require organic principles, often employs them)
>
> Reduction of potable water, natural surface water, and groundwater
>
> Reduction of waste
>
> Recycling of organic matter (though SITES calls this "vegetation trimmings," it is referred to as green waste throughout this book)

Clearly these are all principles discussed in this book (two case studies, Midwest Groundcovers and One Green World, easily meet at least six of these principles). By using the questions included in chapter 8, landscape architects can work to select growers that meet these guidelines and therefore could garner points in this credit. In addition, growers could use this list as a resource for changing practices to become competitive on SITES projects.

- **Prerequisite: Control and retain construction pollutants.** As a prerequisite, this is a must-have, and it primarily deals with erosion and sedimentation control that is often required by local governments. However, it does make note of construction pollutants, including fuels. Though an official "containment plan" needs to be devised and submitted, the additional requirement for spill-reducing fueling (see chapter 3) could provide an additional backup in achieving this prerequisite.

- **Credit: Reuse or recycle vegetation, rocks, and soil generated during construction.** This credit specifically addresses demolished plant material (green waste) as a way to gain up to five points. Though it also addresses soil and rocks (preferring those materials to be reused on-site in a balanced grading plan), the credit specifically mentions recycling of removed vegetation into compost, mulch, erosion protection, and other site elements. Points are only given if 100 percent of plant and soil waste is reused, so composting or recycling of all green waste would be necessary.

- **Credit: Minimize generation of greenhouse gas emissions and exposure to localized air pollutants during construction.** This credit deals directly with construction equipment. It requires a limited idling policy, a preventative maintenance plan for construction vehicles, and the use of ultra-low (15 parts-per-million) sulfur fuel (see chapter 3). It also requires all diesel vehicles to meet Tier 4 emissions rules (see chapter 3) or to take other (after-market) steps to reduce hydrocarbon and nitrogen oxide emissions. Meeting this credit's requirements means that an owner or landscape architect will need to take an active role in working with the installer on what equipment is used on the project. This also means that landscape contractors with newer, efficient equipment will be better positioned to help designers and owners win points under this credit.

- **Prerequisite: Plan for sustainable site maintenance.** This prerequisite requires the creation of a comprehensive long-term maintenance plan that deals with everything from maintenance equipment to historic artifacts to invasive species. Though the plan worksheet does require integrated pest management and encourages composting and recycling of green waste, it does not specifically require certain efficiencies of maintenance equipment or the use of organic fertilizer—merely that equipment and fertilization be considered in the plan. The mere process, however, of creating a maintenance plan at the beginning of a project, especially in the context of an environmental rating exercise, opens the door for landscape architects to recommend and owners to require many of the ideas described in this book for dealing with vehicle fuel, plant pots, irrigation water, organic fertilizer, and green waste.

- **Credit: Recycle organic matter generated during site operations and maintenance.** This idea is covered simply and extensively throughout this book: compost it. Points are available for composting near the site, and more can be gained for composting on-site but only for composting 100 percent of green waste. The credit requires that a plan for recycling "vegetation trimmings" (green waste) be incorporated into the site maintenance plan (see Prerequisite above).

- **Credit: Minimize generation of greenhouse gases and exposure to localized air pollutants during landscape maintenance activities.** Up to four points are available for the use of equipment that either does not use gasoline or meets current EPA final standards for nonroad spark-ignition engines (see chapter 3). This credit tackles dirty mowers, blowers, and trimmers head-on, not by outlawing them, but by, as recommended in this book, requiring that they meet current standards. Management companies, therefore, that have replaced their aging fleets will be at a competitive advantage in SITES projects, and those that have not could be encouraged to do so in order to win a contract on a SITES project.

- **Credit: Monitor performance of sustainable design practices.** Ten points (a significant number) are available for projects willing to monitor, through a third party, performance of the site in meeting certain other credits. Only some credits are eligible for winning points through monitoring, including two of those listed here: the Prerequisite "reduce potable water use for irrigation" and the Credit "protect on-site water sources." Projects willing to empirically study and publish findings on irrigation efficiency or sediment and erosion control (including fuel spillage) could meet the requirements of this credit.

As it should, SITES provides ample opportunity to gain points through environmentally sound, green industry practices. It also empowers landscape architects, as likely managers of the certification process, to require contractors, growers, and management companies to have certain practices in order to be awarded work on a SITES project. Because of the number of credit points that address the green industry's work, it is likely a company or firm would win a SITES certification by performing at least some environmentally sustainable installation, maintenance, or propagation.

Veriflora

Veriflora is the most prominent certification program for cut flowers, potted plants, and peat moss.[4] According to its website, Veriflora has currently certified twenty-one growers of potted plants, trees, and shrubs across the nation (retailers can also become certified, and there are dozens, including major stores, such as ShopKo). A certification allows growers to place the Veriflora logo on pots or on plant tags. The program looks at three broad "elements of sustainability": environmental sustainability, social and economic sustainability, and product integrity. Application to the program is rigorous, and growers must document nearly every nursery practice they undertake. Most notable about this program is the requirement that growers move toward organic pest and disease management and fertilization over time. The program also places significant emphasis on soil health, rather than simply on plant health, and requires an annual statement of how the grower is converting to "organic soil health practices."

In addition, Veriflora producers must address erosion, runoff, habitat protection and mitigation, effects on flora and fauna, energy consumption, product packaging, water use, waste (both hazardous and green), as well as a raft of social and community considerations. Though the program does not immediately require organic practices or a certain energy-reduction target (rather, the producer must document its efforts to reduce energy and become organic), it seems ensured that a Veriflora-certified grower is aware of many of the environmental practices covered in this book.

Using Veriflora to create greener projects

Veriflora, like many certification programs, is designed to give consumers more knowledge and to (hopefully) give environmentally and socially minded producers a competitive advantage. Landscape architects and owners could specify Veriflora-certified nursery stock, if available in your region, just as they would specify wood that is certified by the Forest Stew-ardship Council. Landscape installers could purchase certified plants. The caution here is that the program is still somewhat small, in the context of the nursery industry, and many environmentally minded growers are not certified (including the nurseries profiled in this book). Veriflora is a far more effective brand for the cut-flower market. Most of that product is imported from countries with limited environmental and labor protections, so Veriflora's requirements ensure certain baselines are met—baselines already usually required by law in the United States, where most nursery stock for domestic projects is grown.

At this time, it is probably more useful for landscape architects, owners, installers, and landscape maintenance companies to get to know their growers, and to ask some probing questions about their environmental practices (see "Questions for growers" in chapter 8), rather than to rely solely on Veriflora certification.

USDA organic

Until the U.S. Department of Agriculture officially recognized "organic" as a legally binding food label, the term "organic" could be used however farmers, producers, and marketers wanted.[5] Third-party certification companies were putting their own stamps of approval on products, and each company often had different internal guidelines. The now familiar USDA Organic label has launched an industry worth billions annually, comprising the fastest-growing segment of the grocery industry. The official federal requirements for becoming organic are a bit of a mouthful: "the food or other agricultural product has been produced through approved methods that integrate cultural, biological, and mechanical practices that foster cycling of resources, promote ecological balance, and conserve biodiversity." The key element, though, is that synthetic fertilizers are not permitted.

The term "organic" has found the most traction, of course, with foods (and, more recently, cotton for clothing). But what about nursery plants? In theory, any agricultural product could be certified as organic and sport the round green label. Imagine organic sugarcane ethanol, organic bamboo flooring, or organic vegetable protein packaging materials. Nursery plants could be certified organic, but currently this is exceedingly rare.

Using organic standards to create greener projects

If there were a large number of organically certified nurseries, it would be easy to recommend that owners, management companies, landscape architects, and installers should always specify and purchase organic trees, shrubs, and perennials. This is not, however, the case. Nurseries have not embraced organic certification, likely because so few nurseries are exclusively organic and meeting the USDA's rigorous standards would require an immediate sea change in the total nursery operation. It is also, therefore, counterproductive to push nurseries to pursue this certification. The market (as in the consumer) has not clamored for organic boxwoods as they have for organic bananas.

However, if certified organic plants are available in your region, they are the best guarantee that no synthetic fertilizers were used in the production of those plants.

Salmon-Safe

Based in Portland, Oregon, this ten-year-old certification program[6] deals with only one region—but it's a major region for nursery production: the Pacific Northwest. Oregon and California are two of the top three states for nursery stock production, and Salmon-Safe certifies farms and urban lands there and in Washington and British Columbia. More than 60,000 acres in these areas have been certified to date.

The focus, as evidenced by the name, is to protect watersheds for the various species of Pacific salmon that work their way upstream and inland each year, passing by farms and cities that historically dumped (and, in some cases, currently dump) a wide variety of pollutants into adjacent waters. The program certifies everything from parks and golf courses to urban developments to vineyards to food farms. The nursery program is new and was developed jointly with the Oregon Association of Nurseries (see the case study in chapter 4) and the third-party certifier Food Alliance.

Using Salmon-Safe certification to create greener projects

It's regional and therefore seemingly not applicable to many areas, but plenty of nursery stock comes from Oregon's Willamette Valley and from Northern California, so designers, owners, and green industry professionals nationwide should take note of this program. Salmon-Safe has a long track record of certification, particularly in growing wine, and is now extending that knowledge to nurseries. The primary requirement will be to manage habitat and water quality—something nurseries should do. Simply put, a nursery in salmon country that is not certified or currently pursuing certification should be encouraged to do so, or it should be passed over in favor of those that are. Landscape specifications in the Pacific Northwest could include language to that effect, and specifications elsewhere could require Salmon-Safe certification or in-progress status for any nursery stock that originates in the Pacific Northwest. Because documentation of plant provenance is a typical submittal requirement in most specifications, it would be easy to also document Salmon-Safe certification at the same time.

Over time, more and more nurseries will seek certification, now that there are specific guidelines in place (One Green World was the first nursery to be certified). By making certification a requirement in specifications or for plant materials purchased by owners, the creators and stewards of landscapes can help ensure that the hundreds of thousands of acres of Pacific Northwest nurseries have little impact on local watersheds, water quality, and one of the iconic species of our country.

Living Building Challenge

Operated by the International Living Future Institute, a Pacific Northwest–based nongovernmental organization (NGO), Living Building Challenge is perhaps the most aggressive sustainability certification program in the world.[7] It outlines twenty "imperatives" and four project "typologies" (renovation, landscape and infrastructure, building, and neighborhood).

Though not all twenty imperatives are applicable to every typology, a project must accomplish *all* applicable imperatives to become certified. A landscape project, for instance, must accomplish sixteen imperatives within seven broad areas (called "petals"): site, water, energy, health, materials, equity, and beauty.

This is a tall order, especially considering that there are imperatives requiring that all energy be generated on-site (or sustainably from the surrounding neighborhood), that no off-site potable water be used, and that habitat preservation must be performed in an equal quantity to the developed project area. The central tenet of this program is to measure success based on restorative principles, rather than on code-minimum requirements. This has the effect of only recognizing truly innovative and sustainable projects that go beyond, from an environmental standpoint, any of the other certification systems, including LEED and SITES.

Using the Living Building Challenge to encourage environmental landscape practices

It is important to note here, once again, that this book only describes in detail those items directly related to landscaping. The Living Building Challenge has many imperatives that deal with design, such as Ecological Water Flow, Biophilia, and Beauty. Those Living Building Challenge imperatives that relate directly to landscape installation and maintenance are the following:

- **Imperative 5: Net Zero Water.** The Living Building Challenge requires that all water used on a site should come from captured precipitation or from closed-loop systems. High-efficiency irrigation systems that draw only from gray-water or rainwater catchment cisterns or tanks can help to accomplish this imperative.

- **Imperative 11: Red List.** The "red list," according to the Living Building Challenge, contains materials with serious health and toxicity concerns. The list may be expanded over time, but the current (version 2.0) standard specifically lists petrochemical fertilizers and pesticides. The standard further stresses that such additives may not be used for any initial or ongoing operations and maintenance. Therefore, a fully organic installation and maintenance regime would be necessary in order to achieve Living Building Challenge certification.

- **Imperative 15: Conservation and Reuse.** This imperative deals with material waste and durability during construction and ongoing operations. It requires a written description of how the selection and management of materials, especially reused materials, have influenced and improved a project. All phases of a project must be considered: design, construction, operations, and end of life. Though it is not discussed specifically, the green waste generated during site operations could certainly benefit a project if composted on-site or if composted elsewhere and then returned to nourish the site's soil. Green-waste recycling is certainly in the restorative spirit of the Living Building Challenge and could very well contribute to this imperative. Imperative 15 does, however, require diversion of 100 percent of all soil and biomass waste (green waste) from landfills during the construction phase.

• **Imperative 20: Inspiration and Education.** The Living Building Challenge requires educational content to be made available to the public. The purpose of educational materials, according to the guide, is "to share successful solutions and to motivate others to make change." The exact educational requirements vary by typology, but, for instance, the minimum requirements for a commercial building are an educational website; a public "open day"; a brochure describing the design, environmental features, and site operations; a copy of the operations and maintenance manual; on-site interpretive signage; and a questionnaire to be posted online. Because many of the landscape installation and maintenance ideas described in this book would be right at home in a Living Building Challenge project, and because these ideas are quite rare in general practice, it would be natural to include them in the educational program. Performing and documenting environmentally sound installation and maintenance practices could certainly help accomplish this imperative.

8: Greener Landscape Installation and Maintenance: What to Do Now

As evidenced by rating systems like LEED and SITES and the increased use of environmental technologies like green roofs and rain gardens, landscape architects, owners, and green industry professionals are currently taking great steps forward in environmental stewardship. Most creators and stewards of landscapes are keenly aware of the effect their work has on the environment. They take pains to specify certified wood, to manage storm water, to use recycled materials where available, and to restore landscapes into functioning, healthy ecosystems. Few, however, give much thought to how their landscape plants are grown or how their projects are installed. The tasks involved are a little different for designers, installers, growers, maintainers, and landowners. In all cases, though, this book suggests a fundamental change in how to view the environmental performance of landscapes. It is not enough to create an environmental end product, like a rain garden or green roof; it is equally important to address how a landscape is installed and maintained.

Landscape architects and other designers should rethink their relationships with the growers, installers, and management companies that make their projects possible. Rather than leaving those companies to their own devices—rather than just making sure the end project is sustainable—designers should take a more active role in encouraging greener practices. After all, whether through designs for public bid or selection and recommendation for private projects, landscape architects are important clients of the green industry; as clients, they can ask for or require a certain level of performance. Just as designers recommend and select companies based on workmanship, craftsmanship, and timeliness, it is time to recommend and select companies based on their environmental credibility. Just as plans and specifications require particular aesthetic details, carefully calibrated structural requirements, specific dimensioning, and even certain construction practices, it is time to write into those specifications some environmental requirements governing growers and installers. Just as designers advocate for their own licensure, for federal and state legislation that benefits them, and for local policies that protect water quality and environmental health, it is time landscape architects joined with the green industry to advocate for greener growing, installation, and maintenance practices.

Owners, too, have an important responsibility to green the improvement and maintenance practices associated with their sites. Parks departments, botanical gardens, corporations, universities, and state and federal agencies all manage large tracts of land, sometimes with in-house crews and sometimes with private landscape companies. Owners take great care in selecting private vendors and in maintaining landscapes. It is time they took the same care to select and implement maintenance practices with improved environmental performance. And when initiating new projects—and thereby serving as clients to landscape architects or design-build firms—owners should be at the forefront of including environmental requirements in plans and specifications. As the direct clients to green industry companies and design professionals, owners truly hold all the cards when it comes to how their sites are managed. They should use that power for improved environmental performance.

Growers, installers, and management companies—the green industry itself—can also spearhead environmental practices by changing their own standard operations. The benefit to green industry professionals is that many of these environmental initiatives, like replacing inefficient equipment, reusing water and fertilizer, and utilizing more hand maintenance, can actually save money, both immediately and in the long run. It is not unusual for landscape contractors to maintain small nurseries, where they grow plants to maturity that they have purchased from larger growers. Many also offer design services. Therefore, a green industry professional may cross many trades: a firm may be growing plants that it will install on a project it designed and then will maintain after installation. Because of that turn-key level of service, green industry professionals could have a significant positive impact on the environment at every stage of the landscape installation and management process, simply by changing a few standard practices. In addition, because they work in a much larger industry than landscape architecture (there are more than 1.6 million people employed in the green industry versus fewer than 30,000 landscape architects),[1] growers, installers, and management companies touch more land than designers do. Because of the increased desire by consumers for environmentally sound products, green industry professionals could also leverage their environmental credibility into additional work. The green industry has an excellent name—it's time it started living up to it.

Green industry professionals, landscape architects, and owners have four broad tools of effecting change: plans and specifications, working with green industry professionals, changing internal practices, and advocacy. These can be used in combination to address the five areas of environmental improvement: plant pots, vehicle fuel, energy consumption, water and fertilizer, and green waste. This book has provided some detail on each of these areas of improvement, suggested specific things all creators and stewards of landscapes can do, and shared some case studies about green industry professionals and organizations already working to make a difference. The following sections compile all the preceding recommendations, ideas, and lessons into useful lists that owners, designers, and green industry companies can use when faced with particular tasks, such as evaluating a grower or installer, considering upgrades to facilities, writing environmental requirements into specifications, or considering advocacy initiatives. These lists are tools to place in a toolkit for improving the overall environmental performance of a landscape's installation and ongoing maintenance.

Plans and specifications

Landscape architects and owners can require certain construction practices through plans and written specifications. The following is a list of specific items they should consider writing into specifications for public and private projects or standard agency and organization specifications, in order to require improved environmental performance during installation. Beside each item in parentheses is the area of environmental improvement. The items appear in order of relative ease and importance, with the most critical and easiest-to-implement changes listed first.

❏ Require green-waste composting, by requiring the submittal of drop-off receipts from a composting facility (green waste)
❏ Require plastic recycling by requiring the submittal of drop-off receipts from plastics recyclers or recycling programs (plant pots)
❏ Include a no-idling rule in the project's general conditions (vehicle fuel)
❏ Require spill-reducing fueling systems for on-site fueling (vehicle fuel)
❏ Specify field-grown, balled-and-burlapped trees rather than container-grown plants (plant pots)

- ❏ Specify bare-root plants, wherever appropriate (plant pots)
- ❏ Specify the most advanced irrigation system available, ideally a weather-based system (water and fertilizer)
- ❏ In the initial bids and in the specification, make the installer responsible for maintenance for as long as possible (water and fertilizer)
- ❏ Require construction equipment to comply with current EPA standards (vehicle fuel)
- ❏ Specify organic fertilizers during the project maintenance period (water and fertilizer)
- ❏ Specify that plants materials have Salmon-Safe, USDA organic, or Veriflora certifications, where available and applicable (water and fertilizer)
- ❏ Specify alternatives to plastic plant pots, like biodegradable pots or Ellepots (plant pots)

Questions for growers

Owners and landscape architects occasionally have the opportunity to work directly with growers or nurseries. This is true of design-build firms who purchase plants for installation, but also when design-only firms have projects were plants are custom-grown or where there is a very large volume of plants. Also, owners that regularly change out plant materials, especially annuals, may work directly with a local greenhouse or grower. In these cases, owners and designers have some say in the selection of a grower. Ideally, the owner or designer would visit the grower and see firsthand the environmental practices being employed. But whether the discussion happens in person or by phone or e-mail, the following list provides a framework for determining a grower's environmental credibility.

This is not meant to be a scorecard, because most growers will not be undertaking all of these items, and there are other factors that should drive grower selection. Rather, it is a way for a landscape architect or owner to gather baseline information. It could also be useful (along with the case studies in this book) when suggesting new practices to a grower, either a regular vendor, or one who will be involved in a very large project. Each item is phrased as a question and is followed by a general overview of responses that would indicate good environmental practices. Some items include secondary questions appropriate when an owner or landscape architect is interviewing a potential grower for a custom or large-volume project.

This list is also useful for growers. It generally outlines the key environmental factors in the operation of a nursery operation, so a grower could consider its current answer to each question, then select the items it wants to improve. The idea would be that when a customer—an owner, a landscape installer, or a landscape architect—calls with these questions, the grower has the environmentally sound answer.

❑ **What type of plant pots do you use?**
BEST RESPONSE: recycled plastic, reused pots reclaimed from customers or dumps, or some nonplastic alternative.

CUSTOM GROWER: Have you ever worked with alternatives to plastic, and would you be willing to consider a plastic alternative?

❑ **What do you do with your spent plant pots on site?**
BEST RESPONSE: off-site recycling or reuse after cleaning or steaming.

❑ **Do you accept plastic pots back from installers and other customers for recycling?**
BEST RESPONSE: participates in a regional program or collects and delivers to a recycling facility directly.

❑ **Do you have any initiatives to reduce vehicle fuel use on your site?**
BEST RESPONSE: using nonmotorized transportation for most on-site errands, using biodiesel in larger equipment, using hybrid cars and trucks.

❑ **What energy-efficient features do your greenhouses have?**
BEST RESPONSE: multi-ply plastic sheeting, gasketing around doors, radiant heating

❑ **Are you generating any alternative energy on site?**
BEST RESPONSE: geothermal heating/cooling, solar hot water, solar electric, wind-generated energy

❑ **What other "little things" have you done around your facility to reduce electricity and energy use?**
BEST RESPONSE: lights on motion sensors, higher A/C temperatures and lower heating temperatures, programmable thermostats, focused lighting, compact fluorescent lighting, computer-off policy at the end of the workday.

❑ **How do you irrigate your plants?**
BEST RESPONSE: drip irrigation, rather than overhead spraying.

CUSTOM GROWER: *Do you have a growing field that could be fitted for drip irrigation, and would you be willing to install drip irrigation in the fields where this project's plants are grown?*

❑ **Where does your irrigation water come from?**
BEST RESPONSE: at least some reclaimed from irrigation runoff or collected in cisterns from rainstorms.

❑ **Do you capture your site runoff?**
BEST RESPONSE: captured and reused, captured and infiltrated, or treated through biotic methods before release.

❑ **Do you use conventional or organic fertilizer?**
BEST RESPONSE: organic or an organic/synthetic blend.

CUSTOM GROWER: *Would you be willing to utilize only organic fertilizer for the plants grown for this project and to document that use?*

❑ **How do you control weeds in plant pots and growing fields?**
BEST RESPONSE: mulching, cover crops, hand weeding (as opposed to herbicide application).

CUSTOM GROWER: *Would you be willing to forgo herbicide application in favor of mulching and hand weeding in the fields where this project's plants will be grown, if you were allowed an appropriate increase in price?*

❑ **What do you do with spent soil, plant cuttings, dead plants, and other green waste?**
BEST RESPONSE: composting on-site; transporting to an off-site facility also acceptable

Questions for installers

Designers and owners more frequently have some say over the selection or recommendation of a landscape installer than of a grower. It is not unusual for owners and landscape architects to form regular partnerships with preferred installers, and this can be beneficial to owners (they receive a smoothly run project) and to the environment. In such cases, installers can be encouraged to change their general practices over time—in some, this will even save them money. When looking for new installers to recommend or select, designers and owners should consider environmental performance as one factor in that selection.

The following list of questions can be used in several ways. An owner or designer with an existing relationship with an installer can use the questions and answers to nudge that installer in a more environmental direction. A landscape architect or owner interviewing installers (perhaps even together) can ask these questions, in order to gauge the overall environmental credibility of the contractor. A design-build company might ask these questions of itself, both to determine its general environmental performance or to set goals for improvement. An installation-only company could use this list to improve its own environmental performance, just as a grower might use the list just above.

As with the grower questions, this is not meant as a scorecard but rather as a discussion outline. Also as above, each item is phrased as a question, with preferred answers immediately following.

❏ **Do you recycle plant pots, as a general practice?**
BEST RESPONSE: deliver to recycling facility, or drop off at a collection facility as part of an established recycling program.

❏ **Do you have a no-idling rule at job sites?**
BEST RESPONSE: yes, engines off when loading, unloading, or otherwise not in use

❏ **What types of cars and trucks do your staff drive?**
BEST RESPONSE: the smaller the better for general job-site visits, ideally hybrid or electric cars, also hybrid trucks or biodiesel trucks

❏ **Do you use spill-reducing fueling mechanisms at your own facility and when fueling on-site?**
BEST RESPONSE: yes, every portable gas can should be spill reducing.

❏ **How old is your installation equipment—skidsteers, backhoes, etc.?**
BEST RESPONSE: newer equipment will be generally more fuel efficient and emit less greenhouse gases and particulates, though vehicles meeting Interim Tier 4 or Tier 4 are the gold standard (see chapter 3). Contractors with older vehicles should have a plan in place for replacement, especially in 2013 when all vehicles must comply with Tier 4. Contractors should be asked to provide a list

of their current fleet of equipment, including EPA compliance tiers.

❏ **Are you generating any alternative energy at your facility?**
BEST RESPONSE: geothermal heating/cooling, solar hot water, solar electric, wind.

❏ **What other "little things" have you done around your facility to reduce electricity and energy use?**
BEST RESPONSE: lights on motion sensors, higher A/C temperatures and lower heating temperatures, programmable thermostats, focused lighting, compact fluorescent lighting, computer-off policy at the end of the workday.

❏ **How familiar are you with the latest irrigation technology, like weather-based systems?**
BEST RESPONSE: have installed such systems, or work with a subcontractor with this kind of experience.

❏ **How do you handle green waste collected from project sites, as a general rule?**
BEST RESPONSE: transport to a composting facility.

(Note that this is required in some states, so this question is applicable where composting laws do not exist. See the list in chapter 6.)

Questions for management companies

Far too often, landscape architects take very little responsibility over how their designed landscapes are maintained. This is often because the cost and management of maintenance passes to an owner after construction, and owners can change over time. In some cases, landscape architects may be asked to recommend maintenance companies to owners after the fact, or to consider maintenance and installation as a package. In such cases, just as with the recommendation or selection of a grower or installer, designers should consider the overall environmental credibility of the management company as a facet of their final selection.

In addition, because management companies rely on ongoing business with key clients—both landscape architects and owners—those companies could be encouraged to change their practices over time at the request of those clients. When owners and landscape architects begin work on addition, renovation, or redesign projects on existing sites where there might already be a management company under contract, the opportunity arises to work with that company to make some environmental improvements in maintenance practices.

The following list of items, which is organized in question-response format like those above, can therefore be used in several ways. A landscape architect working with an owner to select a long-term management company can use this list as a guide to discussion of environmental practices. A designer working with an "inherited" management company on an existing project can use this list to discuss, with that company and the owner, ways of improving the environmental performance of the site's management. An owner can use it as guide to selecting a new management company or to working with its existing management company on making environmental improvements. An owner could ask these questions of its in-house maintenance arm, if it has one, as a way to gauge and improve environmental performance. And, as with the previous two lists of questions, a landscape management company could ask these questions of itself, as a way to honestly assess environmental credibility and set a course for improvement.

❑ **Do you recycle plastic pots—those used for replacement plants or for annuals?**
BEST RESPONSE: yes, by delivering them to a plastics recycler or participating in an established recycling program.

❑ **Have you considered using alternatives to plastic, especially for annual plants?**
BEST RESPONSE: use of Ellepots® or biodegradable vegetable fiber pots.

❑ **Do you have a no-idling rule at job sites, as a general rule?**
BEST RESPONSE: yes, engines off when loading, unloading, or otherwise not in use

❑ **What types of cars and trucks do your staff drive?**
BEST RESPONSE: the smaller the better for general job site visits, ideally hybrid or electric cars, also hybrid trucks or biodiesel trucks.

❑ **Do you use spill reducing fueling mechanisms when fueling on site?**
BEST RESPONSE: yes, every can is spill reducing.

❑ **How old is your maintenance equipment—mowers, blowers, trimmers, etc.?**

BEST RESPONSE: handheld small engine equipment should be 2007 model year or newer, since that is the year the latest EPA emissions rules went into effect. Mowers should be model years 2011 or 2012, depending on the type of mower (see chapter 3).

❏ **Do you have a plan for phasing out older equipment?**
BEST RESPONSE: should have a plan in place to gradually retire equipment that does not meet current EPA standards.

❏ **Are you performing come maintenance tasks, like pruning and leaf removal, by hand?**
BEST RESPONSE: yes, some maintenance tasks are performed by hand, without motorized equipment, as standard practice.

❏ **Would you consider performing some maintenance tasks by hand, if you could increase costs to cover it?**
BEST RESPONSE: should be able to provide cost differential between machine and hand maintenance, taking into account reduced equipment maintenance and fuel costs.

❏ **Are you generating any alternative energy at your facility?**
BEST RESPONSE: geothermal heating/cooling, solar hot water, solar electric, wind.

❏ **What other "little things" have you done around your facility to reduce electricity and energy use?**
BEST RESPONSE: lights on motion sensors, higher A/C temperatures and lower heating temperatures, programmable thermostats, focused lighting, compact fluorescent lighting, computer-off policy at the end of the work day.

❏ **Are you familiar with organic maintenance practices and would you consider using them?**
BEST RESPONSE: already using organic fertilizers and pest control, including compost tea, or currently working to find the best organic solution for their business or facility.

❏ **How familiar are you with the latest irrigation technology, like weather-based systems?**
BEST RESPONSE: have installed such systems, or work with a subcontractor with this kind of experience.

❑ **How do you handle green waste collected from project sites, as a general rule?**

BEST RESPONSE: transport to a composting facility. (Note that this is required in some states, so this question is applicable where composting laws do not exist. See the list in chapter 6.)

Advocacy ideas

Advocacy, of course, requires more energy—sometimes a lot more energy—than asking a few questions or writing some new lines into a specification. Nevertheless, landscape architects, owners, and green industry professionals are often called upon to take positions on issues of the day, to volunteer time for causes, and to lead or support proposals for new rules, laws, and ordinances. Because all these creators and stewards of landscapes tend to be attuned to environmental causes, advocacy for greater environmental performance suits them well.

And the different groups of landscape professionals will rarely be alone in such advocacy. As evidenced by the Minnesota Nursery and Landscape Association, the Oregon Association of Nurseries, and other organizations, the green industry itself sees the need for change. Green industry organizations, however, are inherently shackled by a diverse group of members, many of whom may not want additional rules that they perceive may cut into their profit margin. When green industry organizations and design professional organizations team up, however, that can provide an additional push by convincing growers, installers, and managers that their clients do, in fact, want better environmental performance—and that such improved performance may not cost a lot of money.

Types and methods of advocacy will vary significantly by region, depending on the laws already in place, the current mind-set of the local industry, and simple practicality. The following list describes the key items for which landscape professionals should advocate. Each item is phrased to relate an environmentally sound stance. Bullets beneath the statement suggest specific ways designers, owners, and green industry professionals might work to accomplish that stance. The bullets are organized in order of the least effort to the most effort.

❑ **Recycle plastic plant pots as a standard practice.**
- Learn about existing recycling programs, so that information is always on hand when you are asked by clients, contractors, friends, or neighbors.
- Participate, on a volunteer basis, in an existing recycling

program, with publicity, delivery of pots to a recycling facility, or collection-day staffing.

- Work to include recycling requirements into the standard specifications of an agency or government.
- Establish a recycling program, in partnership with other organizations, foundations, nonprofits, and so on.

❑ **Increase fuel efficiency and reduce emissions for all engines.**
- Support and lobby for more stringent standards when they are proposed by state and federal governments.

❑ **For landscape management companies, use the most efficient maintenance equipment available.**
- Incentivize the replacement of older equipment compliant with EPA small engine or Tier 4 diesel standards, either through an organizational buy-back program, through education on cost savings of upgrades, or through contingent recommendations.

❑ **Compost all green waste.**
- Work to include composting requirements into the standard specifications of an agency or government, where composting laws do not exist.

- Support and lobby for state and regional laws and policies forbidding the transport of green waste to landfills.

Absent from this advocacy list are specific stances on energy consumption and water and fertilizer use (including organic maintenance). The reason for this is that these are "sea change" items often embroiled in national and worldwide dialogues. General advocacy for energy efficiency, alternative fuels and energy, efficient water use, environmental pollutants, and fossil-fuel reduction will have an inherent effect on the green industry. However, there is nothing specific to be done relative to improving this industry, as opposed to improving global conditions as a whole.

Of utmost importance is that the creators and stewards of landscapes gain a better understanding of each other: how they function, what their challenges are, how they make money. Landscape architects and the green industry, in particular, should more closely ally themselves, so that designers don't become just rule makers but partners in change.

At times, designers and owners will have to mandate change. But most often they should use existing relationships with growers, contractors, and management companies to help those companies improve environmental performance and, in many cases, save themselves money. Improved environmental performance does not necessarily cost more money, not up front and not in the long run, and this fact should be made clear by owners and landscape architects when they discuss such initiatives with green industry professionals.

Above all, as stated at the beginning of this chapter, if creators and stewards of landscapes hope to lead truly environmentally sound projects, they must take more control over the environmental credibility not just of their built works, but of how their works get built.

CASE STUDY: MESA DESIGN GROUP

Fred Walters feels that most installation and maintenance specifications were established by contractors for their own convenience. Walters is a principal of the Dallas-based landscape architecture firm MESA Design Group, which boasts a diverse portfolio of projects ranging from small residences to parks to massive planning projects across the world. Walters says it isn't that unusual for homeowners to question the use of synthetic fertilizers and harmful pesticides and herbicides, but that such concern was rare for those who planned public or corporate projects. About ten years ago, prompted by a municipal project in the Dallas suburb of Irving, MESA began considering incorporating organic soil preparation and maintenance into all its projects.

The firm started with research. It looked at the costs of maintenance and tried to find a financial reason for cities or corporations to buy into an organic regime. MESA also began finding ways to incorporate organic maintenance into its standard specifications and maintenance recommendations. "This can't be about just loading phosphorous and nitrogen on a site," says

Walters. Instead, for MESA, an organic regime begins with the soil. A typical MESA specification and bid package includes a requirement for the contractor to sample the soil in multiple locations and send the soil for analysis to a specialty lab that can make organic treatment recommendations. Walters cautions that this is a key part of the process. A typical soil lab will produce "basically a geotechnical report." Some MESA-required testing goes to Soil Foodweb Oregon, a specialty "biological agriculture" lab in Corvallis, Oregon, while some stays near home at Texas Plant Soil Labs. The cost of the testing is built into the bid, as is an allowance for soil amendments.

Once organic recommendations are made by the lab, the contractor is bound to provide those amendments, which are generally mixed in during planting-bed preparation, as usual. Instead, though, of synthetic fertilizers, pre-emergent herbicides, and moisture retention mumbo-jumbo, the additives might include molasses, acid humus, sand, or other organic materials.

Of course, MESA doesn't always get its way, and Walters admits his company's standard specifications and recommendations are a starting point. He says it's ultimately up to the client. "You have to work on them, and work on them, and work on them," he stresses. "It's a battle."

Convincing a client is especially critical for ongoing organic maintenance. "That's every landscape architect's dilemma," says Walters, because designers can provide recommendations but can only ask a manager to "pretty please" don't use synthetic fertilizer, unless the owner is completely on board. And what's particularly difficult is that organic preparation and maintenance can cost more up front—the savings are on the back end, when the landscape really takes off and thrives on its own because the soil is healthy.

When asked what other landscape architects and owners can do to encourage greener practices, Walters recommends three tasks. First, find contractors, growers, and nurseries that are already doing these things. Several of those are profiled in this book, and this chapter provides a list of questions owners and designers can ask green industry professionals in order to glean their environmental commitment. Second, find people in the local region who are exploring the cutting edge of organics. MESA worked with the local organic guru Howard Garrett (the Dirt Doctor) when it created its specification—probably part of the reason for the emphasis on the soil. Lastly, get to the site at the critical phases of construction: soil testing, initial grading, soil amendment addition, topsoil spreading. Walters recommends working some key earthwork-related visits into the construction observation contract. "At the end of the day," he says, "contractors want to do a good job but may not know how," especially when faced with unfamiliar specification language. Not only do landscape contractors want guidance, says Walters, but it is also an excellent learning experience to see how projects get installed—to see if a project is being (or, in reality, can be) put in the ground as anticipated.

Afterword/About the Website

The eight case studies included in this book provide an overview of a variety of environmentally sound landscaping practices. They do not represent, of course, the only nurseries, landscape installation and maintenance companies, and landscape architects working to improve the environmental performance of their landscapes. Even as this book was in preparation, I began to learn of other companies that could have deserved a place in these pages.

In an effort to provide additional resources to readers and to continue to learn from those with real-world experience, I am complementing the book with a website identifying additional case studies. GreeningtheLandscapeBook.com serves as a clearing-house for state-of-the-art examples from around the nation and across professions. On the site are company descriptions and photos of innovative environmental landscaping practices, arranged by category of environmental impact—just like this book. They are also arranged geographically, to help you more easily find companies in your area.

None of these companies or organizations paid to be included. I selected them based on the principles set forth in this book.

In the spirit of expanding the community of environmentally sound landscaping, I invite readers to share your own practices with me, for possible inclusion in GreeningtheLandscapeBook.com. If you operate, work for, or know of a nursery, landscape company, parks department, college campus, public agency, or landscape architecture firm that is working to mitigate the environmental impacts of landscapes, you can visit the website GreeningtheLandscapeBook.com to find out about becoming a featured case study.

With each new idea the greening of the landscape takes another step forward. Go to GreeningtheLandscapeBook.com to learn more. I look forward to hearing about your own efforts.

Notes

General Notes

All information included in the main text and in the case studies about Christy Webber Landscapes, Lambert Landscape Company, MESA Design Group, Midwest Groundcovers, the Minnesota Nursery and Landscape Association, One Green World, the Oregon Association of Nurseries, and Pacific Landscape Management is based on personal communications between 2009 and 2011.

Information on general nursery, installation, maintenance, and landscape architectural practices comes from personal experience and personal communications with industry professionals since 1998.

Chapter 1

1. Personal communication, 2009.
2. All emissions and efficiency data come from the Environmental Protection Agency. The EPA's small engine program is at www.epa.gov/otaq/equip-ld.htm. The nonroad diesel program is at www.epa.gov/nonroad-diesel/.
3. United States Composting Council, at compostingcouncil.org/current-alerts-and-campaigns/.

Chapter 2

1. www.monrovia.com.
2. www.eastjordanplastics.com/plastic-recycling.html.
3. http://en.wikipedia.org/wiki/Peat.
4. www.veriflora.com.
5. www.cowpots.com.
6. http://ecoforms.com.
7. www.rossosinternational.com.
8. www.rushcreekdesigns.com.
9. www.ellepot.dk.

Chapter 3

1. See chapter 1, note 2.
2. In addition to the EPA data cited above, a useful resource for understanding nonroad diesel rules is the Emissions Hub (http://www.johndeereemissionshub.com), operated by the equipment maker John Deere. Through a company blog, a company representative explains the EPA rules in understandable and accurate language. A particularly good post on Tier 4 and Interim Tier 4 occurred on January 9, 2011, at http://www.johndeereemissionshub.com/2011/01/09/interim-tier-4-101-how-we-got-here-and-what-it-means-to-you/.
3. Ted Steinberg, *American Green: The Obsessive Quest for the Perfect Lawn* (New York: W.W. Norton & Company, 2006), 8.
4. www.nospill.com
5. www.rainbird.com/landscape/products/controllers/ETmanager.htm

Chapter 4

1. Personal communication and site visit, May 2009; personal communication, September 2011; Adam Regn Arvidson, "A Greener Green Industry," *Landscape Architecture*, June 2010.
2. The U.S. Department of Energy operates the Energy Savers website, which provides basic information on geothermal and other energy systems. The geothermal section is at www.energysavers.gov/your_home/space_heating_cooling/index.cfm/mytopic=12640.

Chapter 5

1. Bryan Walsh, "Tropicana: Trying to Make a Greener Orange Juice," *Time*, March 11, 2010. Also available online at www.time.com/time/magazine/article/0,9171,1978783,00.html.
2. Personal communication, March 2011.
3. The site www.dirtdoctor.com provides various resources on organic gardening and landscape maintenance.
4. Adam Regn Arvidson, "Green X 3," *Landscape Architecture*, May 2011.

Chapter 6

1. The best source for the state of composting laws nationwide is the U.S. Composting Council (www.compostingcouncil.org). This website provides information on current composting campaigns, current laws, and composting facilities nationwide.
2. Personal communication, June 2011.
3. U.S. Composting Council.
4. U.S. Composting Council (www.compostingcouncil.org/current-alerts-and-campaigns/landfill-ban-map-5-2011/), after Haaren, Themelis, and Goldstein, "State of Garbage in America," *BioCycle*, October 2010.

Chapter 7

1. All LEED information is found on the U.S. Green Building Council website, www.usgbc.org/DisplayPage.aspx?CategoryID=19

2. LEED Canada can be found at the Canada Green Building Council's site, www.cagbc.org.

3. All SITES information can be found at www.sustainablesites.org.

4. www.veriflora.com

5. Visit www.udsa.gov, pull down "Programs and Services," and click on National Organic Program."

6. www.salmonsafe.org and http://foodalliance.org

7. https://ilbi.org

Chapter 8

1. In 2002 the U.S. Census Bureau reported 753,557 jobs in horticultural services (which include landscape architecture jobs) and another 910,104 jobs in wholesale and retail sales, as reported by the American Nursery and Landscape Association (www.anla.org/index.cfm?area=&page=Content&CategoryID=164). Conversely, in 2008 there were 26,700 landscape architects, according to the Bureau of Labor Statistics (www.bls.gov/k12/nature02.htm). Of these, 15,000 were licensed, according to the American Society of Landscape Architects (www.asla.org/FAQAnswer.aspx?CategoryTitle=About the Profession&Category=3150#DispID3134).

Green Industry Companies

Christy Webber Landscapes
2900 West Ferdinand Street
Chicago, IL 60612
(773) 533-0477
www.christywebber.com

Lambert Landscape Company
(including Moore Life and Moore Tree Care)
6333 Denton Drive, #100
Dallas, TX 75235
(214) 350-8350
www.lamberts.net

Midwest Groundcovers
P.O. Box 748
St. Charles, IL 60174
(847) 742-1790
www.midwestgroundcovers.com

Minnesota Nursery and
Landscape Association
1813 Lexington Ave. N
Roseville, MN 55113
651-633-4987
www.mnla.biz

One Green World
28696 South Cramer Road
Molalla, OR 97038
(503) 651-3005
www.onegreenworld.com

Oregon Association of Nurseries
29751 SW Town Center Loop W.
Wilsonville, OR 97070
(800) 342-6401
www.oan.org

Pacific Landscape Management
21555 NW Amberwood Drive
Hillsboro, OR 97124
(503) 648-3900
www.pacscape.com

Index